THE COLUMBIA ICEFIELD

Mount Athabasca
and neighbouring
peaks of the Columbia
Icefield region.

THE COLUMBIA ICEFIELD

3rd Edition

by

Robert William Sandford

EPCOR Chair, Water Security,
United Nations University Institute
for Water, Environment and Health

RMB

RMB | Rocky Mountain Books Ltd.
rmbooks.com
@rmbooks
facebook.com/rmbooks

Cataloguing data available from Library and Archives Canada

ISBN 978-1-77160-154-2 (paperback)

Printed and bound in Canada by Friesens

Distributed in Canada by Heritage Group Distribution and in the U.S. by Publishers Group West

For information on purchasing bulk quantities of this book, or to obtain media excerpts or invite the author to speak at an event, please visit rmbooks.com and select the "Contact Us" tab.

RMB | Rocky Mountain Books is dedicated to the environment and committed to reducing the destruction of old-growth forests. Our books are produced with respect for the future and consideration for the past.

We acknowledge the financial support of the Government of Canada through the Canada Book Fund and the Canada Council for the Arts, and of the province of British Columbia through the British Columbia Arts Council and the Book Publishing Tax Credit.

Disclaimer
The actions described in this book may be considered inherently dangerous activities. Individuals undertake these activities at their own risk. The information put forth in this guide has been collected from a variety of sources and is not guaranteed to be completely accurate or reliable. Many conditions and some information may change owing to weather and numerous other factors beyond the control of the authors and publishers. Individuals or groups must determine the risks, use their own judgment, and take full responsibility for their actions. Do not depend on any information found in this book for your own personal safety. Your safety depends on your own good judgment based on your skills, education, and experience.

It is up to the users of this guidebook to acquire the necessary skills for safe experiences and to exercise caution in potentially hazardous areas. The authors and publishers of this guide accept no responsibility for your actions or the results that occur from another's actions, choices, or judgments. If you have any doubt as to your safety or your ability to attempt anything described in this guidebook, do not attempt it.

*For visitors from Canada and
all over the world who come to see
the glory of the Columbia Icefield, and for
the scientists who give meaning and
value to the experience.*

Saskatchewan Glacier.

All photos are by R.W. Sandford except those noted otherwise.

CONTENTS

A digital elevation model of the Columbia
Icefield created by the Geological Survey of
Canada's glaciology section.

The view that lay before us in the
evening light was one that does not often
fall to the lot of modern mountaineers.
A new world was spread at our feet: to
the westward stretched a vast ice-field
probably never before seen by the human
eye, and surrounded by entirely unknown,
unnamed and unclimbed peaks.

—J. Norman Collie upon discovering the
Columbia Icefield, 1898

Welcome to the Columbia Icefield

By any standard, the Columbia Icefield is a stunning geographical feature. It is a high basin of accumulated snow and ice that straddles some 220 square kilometres, roughly 85 square miles, of the Great Divide separating British Columbia from Alberta along the spine of the Rocky Mountains. Located at 52° north latitude and 117° west longitude, it has long been incorrectly touted locally as the largest concentration of glacial ice below the Arctic Circle in North America. What is true, however, is that the Columbia is the largest of the numerous icefields that straddle the Continental Divide of North America. It is one of the last places in southern Canada

Athabasca Glacier and the Columbia Icefield.

where cold, wind, weather and water still interact in exactly the same way they did during the last ice age. But what makes this icefield truly unique is its accessibility.

At Athabasca Glacier in Jasper National Park, you can literally get out of your car and, in just a few moments, walk directly back into the Pleistocene, a colder epoch in the Earth's history when much of North America was buried 2 kilometres deep in ice. One is immediately stood upright by the cold wind blowing off the thick ice. Melting at the glacier's snout is snow that fell and was compressed into ice 400 years ago. The towering black peaks seem to lean over you. The familiar sun is a cold and distant star.

There is a different sense of time here. Fleeting hours hardly matter. The day seems the smallest unit, the season next, then the year. Beyond the year there is only the timelessness of epochs, the incomprehensibly vast passing of the geological seasons, mountains rising and falling, and the coming and going of entire rafts of planetary life. Confronted by eternity, we feel small before the grumbling ice. Epiphany is possible here, a sense of aesthetic arrest. A shudder runs through your soul as you realize, suddenly, what an ice age really is.

Few who visit the Columbia Icefield today fail to be impressed by the kinds of conditions that existed during the last ice age. It was a different and very dangerous world we emerged from. The ease of access is beguiling, however. To be at the terminus of Athabasca Glacier during peak melt is to understand the full extent to which glaciation reshaped the North American continent. If you give in to the mind-slowing scale of the high mountain landscape and wait long enough, the

The Sunwapta River emerges from the snout of Athabasca Glacier.

groaning and pinging of the advancing ice can actually be heard. This is not just the sound the glacier makes as it grumbles toward the valley floor; this is the sound that ice has been making for the more than three million years that glaciers have been pouring forth from the Columbia Icefield during the last lingering age of ice in the northern hemisphere. But there is far more to hear than just the echo of ice scraping across bedrock. There is the sound of water, too. On any given summer day, meltwater flows over almost the entire surface of the glacier. The water accumulates into surficial streams which plunge deep into the glacier by way of crevasses and millwells that channel the waters to the bottom of the glacier. Melt from the surface, in tandem

with streams that flow out from under the snout of the glacier, collects briefly into a small lake before spilling out to become the headwaters of the Sunwapta River, a major tributary of the Athabasca River. What we witness at the terminus of Athabasca Glacier is nothing less than the birth of a life-giving watercourse that has flowed without interruption for more than 10,000 years. But this privileged access to timelessness and the primacy of the past is not without hazard. The terminus of Athabasca Glacier is a dynamic and treacherous place.

Visiting the Columbia Icefield

Straddling Banff and Jasper national parks in the heart of the UNESCO Canadian Rocky Mountain Parks World Heritage Site, the icefield can be easily reached by car by way of excellent highways from any of western Canada's major cities. What is amazing about this easy access is that it makes it possible for the average person to simply open a door into a not-so-distant time in the Earth's history when our planet's climate was different: when it was colder and much of North America was covered by ice so deep that it altered the character of the landscapes over which it flowed. During this epoch there was so much ice on the land that sea levels were dramatically reduced globally. The resulting climate was such that it altered the evolutionary course of almost every species of life on Earth, including our own. This, however, is a climate to which we are no longer well adapted.

A qualified mountain guide takes a group on a tour of major surface features of the Athabasca Glacier.
PHOTOGRAPH COURTESY OF ATHABASCA GLACIER ICEWALKS

Legendary Columbia Icefield Icewalks guide Bernard Faure at the terminus of the Athabasca Glacier. The margins of lateral moraines at the terminus of any big glacier can be particularly hazardous because of both rockfall from above and the unpredictable collapse of unstable, debris-covered ice beneath the moraine. Faure will not permit even experienced climbers in his group to approach dangerous features such as collapsing moraines on Athabasca Glacier any closer than is safe.

While it is easy to experience the awe, few of us have any idea of exact nature of the hazards until they are explained to us or we blunder into them accidentally. Because visitors are frequently not adequately equipped, don't heed warning signs and don't know how to identify hazards, accidents are not uncommon on Athabasca Glacier. Even very experienced mountaineers are extremely careful on and around the snout of Athabasca Glacier. Nearly continuous rockfall caused by frost-shattering on steep mountain walls surrounding

While glaciers are always unpredictable, there are safe ways to travel on the Columbia Icefield. A modicum of caution and good sense can significantly reduce your chances of being hurt in unfamiliar terrain and circumstances. Things to consider include the following:

1. **The most obvious and most often ignored safety tip** is to stay off the ice, especially at the terminus of Athabasca Glacier. Anyone who is not a mountaineer or experienced in glacier travel should not venture onto the ice without an expert guide. From April until well into July, most of the glacier and all of the icefield proper is covered with the previous winter's snow, which forms insubstantial bridges over crevasses. These bridges can be very difficult to detect, and they may collapse under a person's weight. When the winter snow is gone, the crevasses are easier to avoid, but the ice is extremely slippery in some places and jaggedly sharp in others. Injuries caused by simply falling and sliding on the ice are common and can be quite serious.

2. **It is not just the ice** that can be dangerous. Walking up moraines – the debris slopes on the sides and at the terminus of the glacier – can be like trying to walk on marbles that are rolling over a rock surface. It is important to understand that the entire Columbia Icefield area is in constant flux and very little of it remains in anything close to a permanent geophysical state for long. Even the largest boulders sometimes move. Straying from trails is not advised.

3. **Bring warm clothes** and wear sturdy shoes or boots that provide good traction. Weather in the Columbia Icefield region is highly unpredictable and can change very rapidly. Even in midsummer you have to be prepared for bitter cold. Summer winds off the ice can be bone-chilling, even if you are dressed for winter.

4. **Keep children in sight** and under control. While landscape experiences of the kind the Columbia Icefield offers can be especially transformative for a child, Athabasca Glacier is not like your backyard or a playground. It is a dynamic part of the Earth system in which many of the most powerful forces of nature interact and must be respected as such.

5. **To protect people** you may not see below you, do not throw rocks or push any down steep moraines. Once even small rocks hit the glacier's surface they can begin bouncing down the ice, creating a potentially fatal hazard for others.

the ice is a serious hazard. It is not uncommon for head-sized rocks to come bouncing and whistling down the glacier, especially near the snout. There are also many tragic stories of people in street shoes who have slipped on the ice and fallen unroped into crevasses from which it was impossible to rescue them before they died right before the eyes of loved ones.

One such story is particularly horrendous. A family drove to the terminus of the glacier and walked together up to the ice. Perhaps because of their awe or because there were so many others doing the same, they walked past the signs posted by Parks Canada warning visitors of the hazards, and stepped right onto the ice. Seeing others walking in the area above them, the father and son continued on. Suddenly the son disappeared. Quickly making his way to where the boy had vanished, the father found his son wedged below in a crevasse. Try as he might, he could not reach the boy. He called a nearby mountain guide who was leading a group of sightseers kept tightly together on a climbing rope. The guide also tried to reach the boy but was unable to do so. The guide was able finally to get a rope around the child but was unable to gain the leverage necessary to pull him out of the crevasse. A national park rescue team was summoned.

It was an hour and a half before the boy was finally pulled from the crevasse. By that time, however, contact with the ice has cooled the core temperature of his body. He was already hypothermic and soon died. A legal battle ensued during which the aggrieved family sought to lay responsibility for the death of their son on Parks Canada. Parks, however, was found not responsible. It was an unfortunate momentary lapse of human judgment, together with the blind coldness of the indifferent ice, that killed the child. As this story demonstrates, anyone wishing to visit Athabasca Glacier should bring with them a profound respect for the ice and be aware of its treacherousness at all times. They should also pay attention to signs.

Athabasca Glacier Icewalks

Guides from Athabasca Glacier Icewalks have been leading people across the glaciers of the Columbia Icefield since 1985. That was the year when a young assistant ski guide by the name of Peter Lemieux decided to offer people the opportunity to explore Athabasca Glacier on foot. Peter had worked as an interpreter for Parks Canada, the national parks service, for a number of years and knew there was great interest from travellers. The Icewalk was born. Since that time, the company has led thousands of people safely across the glacier.

Peter Lemieux established Athabasca Glacier Icewalks in 1985.
PHOTO COURTESY OF ATHABASCA GLACIER ICEWALKS

Athabasca Glacier Icewalks guides come from around the world to lead trips here: from Canada, New Zealand, Iceland, all places with extensive glaciers. The guides are trained in glaciology, safe glacier travel and advanced first aid. They also know a great deal about the natural and human history of Athabasca Glacier and the Columbia Icefield. Their aim is to make your trip onto the glacier the safest and most enjoyable possible, and to share their passion for one of nature's great wonders. It's a perfect place to gain an in-depth understanding of active glaciation.

The Columbia Icefield "Ice Explorer" experience

With the coming of the Great Depression in 1931, the Rocky Mountain national parks were chosen as sites for relief projects that offered unemployed men opportunities to work on construction projects financed by the federal government. The largest of these was the construction of the Jasper–Banff highway. When a paved road along what had been called "this wonder trail" opened in 1940, it was hailed as a modern engineering marvel. But it soon became clear that it wasn't the road itself that was the attraction. The landscape through which the "Highway in the Clouds" wandered was immediately recognized as some of the most spectacular in the country. According to many, the most amazing part of the highway was the slow climb up the steep slopes of Sunwapta Pass to the snout of Athabasca Glacier, the only major outflow of the Columbia Icefield accessible by road. In order to accommodate motorists travelling to the glacier and beyond, the government let a tender for the development of a small chalet overlooking the great expanse of slowly moving ice. The Columbia Icefield Chalet was built in 1939 by Brewster Transport, a well-established Banff sightseeing company that would later also take over the commercial tour operation on the glacier.

COLUMBIA ICEFIELD CHALET

A postcard featuring the first Icefield Chalet, circa 1939, shows the extent of Athabasca Glacier about 75 years before this book was written.

Prior to the completion of this gravel road, only hardened adventurers had ever seen Athabasca Glacier or the Columbia Icefield. After the highway officially opened in 1940, the idea of mechanized public transportation on the readily accessible glacier began to take hold.

In 1946 an army half-track left over from the Second World War made its appearance on the ice by way of the glacier's gently sloped terminus. In 1948 a man named Alex Watt began offering tours on the glacier using half-tracks, a project that succeeded well enough to draw the attention of Canada's National Parks Service, which later granted a concession licence for such an operation. Much to Watt's disappointment, a Jasper entrepreneur named Bill Ruddy was awarded the official government-authorized concession for the motorized Columbia Icefield attraction in 1952. It was Ruddy who introduced the famous six-passenger Bombardier snowmobile to the surface of the glacier and made the tour famous around the world.

By 1951 the toe of the glacier was becoming so steep that vehicles had trouble ascending it. By the mid-'50s, after lengthy negotiations, the federal government agreed to build a road along the south moraine of Athabasca Glacier. For years it was from this moraine that snow machines inched their way down onto the surface of the glacier. When upgrading of the Banff–Jasper Highway from oiled gravel surface to a modern paved highway was completed in 1961, traffic up what by then was known as the "Wonder Road" increased dramatically. More and more visitors wanted to visit Athabasca Glacier so they could touch the ice of the only road-accessible outflow of the famous Columbia Icefield.

By 1968 Ruddy had 20 snowmobiles on the ice and a summer staff of over a hundred at the Columbia Icefield. The Ruddys were one busy family. Too busy. In 1969 Bill Ruddy sold Snowmobile Tours Limited to Brewster Transportation & Tours, which already owned the Columbia Icefield Chalet.

In purchasing the Athabasca Glacier snowmobile operation, Brewster was immediately confronted with the challenge of developing a more reliable technology for transporting larger numbers of visitors onto the glacier in a safe and efficient manner. The Bombardier snow machines they purchased with the business were reaching the end of their practical life. Though the Bombardier was fun to ride in, it was noisy, rough-riding and expensive to maintain. Moreover, because each machine could carry only six to eight passengers, the snowmobile fleet could not keep up with the long lines of people who wanted to experience the surface of the ice.

A restored Bombardier snowmobile of the kind used for decades on Athabasca Glacier is on display outside the Columbia Icefield Visitor Centre. Its limitation was that it could only carry six to eight passengers.

Heavy visitation at the glacier and a new focus on group tour travel made larger vehicles a necessity. Brewster responded by experimenting with machines that featured bus bodies attached to track mechanisms that had been developed for Arctic exploration. The next stage in the evolution of the snow coach was a custom-made coach body attached to a much-improved track system.

The realization that even the best-designed tracked vehicles caused unacceptable disturbance to the surface of the glacier led to experimentation with all-terrain vehicles with large, low-pressure tires. This technology was tested first in the Arctic and found to be far more efficient and environmentally friendly than earlier track technology.

"Shake and Bake": The next iteration of Athabasca Glacier motorized transportation was a coach body on tracks. This vehicle provided neither a smooth ride nor air conditioning, hence its nickname.

The Foremost Terra Bus, or Snowcoach ("Snocoach" as Brewster spelled it), was developed jointly by Brewster and Canadian Foremost in Calgary, Alberta. Later models were renamed "Ice Explorers." Though very expensive, these remarkable 20-tonne, 56-passenger machines have proven to be ideal vehicles for glacier travel, especially when operated by well-trained driver-guides. It had taken 20 years for Brewster to perfect transportation technology that would work in the fragile and difficult terrain of the Columbia Icefield. The company's fleet of "Ice Explorers" now take as many as half a million people a year onto the surface of Athabasca Glacier.

Brewster's Columbia Icefield "Ice Explorers" at the turn-around halfway up Athabasca Glacier.

10 POPULAR QUESTIONS ABOUT THE COLUMBIA ICEFIELD

1. Is it Columbia "Icefield" or Columbia "Icefields"?

Because the Columbia Icefield is a high-altitude basin in which snowfall collects and from which a number of glaciers flow, it is considered a single geological feature. Thus Columbia "Icefield" is a singular term, while "Icefields" Parkway is plural because more than one icefield can be viewed along its course.

2. How big is the Columbia Icefield?

This is an interesting question. It was widely held for decades that the field was about 325 square kilometres in extent. This was the area reported in earlier editions of this book. The origins of this estimate appear to go back to a map in a 38-page publication entitled *Geology of the National Parks in the Rockies and Selkirks*, published by the Canadian Government Travel Bureau, Department of Resources and Development in 1952. The map, albeit only a sketch, clearly depicts the inclusion of the Clemenceau and Chaba icefields but erroneously charts these as being the Columbia Icefield. What is interesting is that it was generally held at the time that given its altitude the area of the icefield would not significantly change over time. Recent satellite analyses, however, indicate that what can properly be defined as the Columbia was approximately 223 square kilometres, or about 86 square miles, in 2005. The decade that followed was among the warmest on record, though, which means the Columbia Icefield would have shrunk even further at its margins and will likely continue to do so.

For decades it was maintained that the Columbia Icefield was the largest non-polar ice mass in North America. We now know this is not the case. The Andrei Icefield, north of Stewart, BC, is larger, as is the Seward-Bering icefield system in coastal Alaska. Several other icefields in the Coast Mountains are also larger. The neighbouring "Clemenceau Icefield" could also be larger, though in fact glaciologists now view it as more of a group of glaciers with multiple ridge lines and flow divides than as a single icefield. The Columbia Icefield is hardly insubstantial, however. It is the largest of the numerous icefields that straddle the Continental Divide in North America.

3. Are all the glaciers in the Canadian Rockies retreating?

While some tidewater glaciers in the higher latitudes of the northern hemisphere may grow in size if warming temperatures increase winter precipitation, almost all the glaciers in the Canadian Rockies appear to be in a prolonged period of recession. Recent research, in fact, suggests that as many as 300 glaciers disappeared along the Great Divide in the Canadian Rockies between 1920 and 2005. Only pocket glaciers high on north-facing walls of big mountains appear to be unaffected by warming valley temperatures.

4. How deep is the ice?

According to the Geological Survey of Canada, the upper icefield – that is, the part of the icefield around the outlet valley glaciers – varies in depth from about 150 to 300 metres, with some limited regions too deep to measure using radar. From theoretical considerations, however, the maximum depth of the icefield may exceed 500 to 600 metres. The depth of Athabasca Glacier as measured in 1990 at its deepest point, which happens to be at the turnaround for the "Ice Explorers" touring its surface, was roughly 300 metres, or nearly 1,000 feet. Downwasting

An Athabasca Glacier Icewalks guide leads a group beneath the spectacular icefalls at the headwall of Athabasca Glacier. PHOTO COURTESY OF ATHABASCA GLACIER ICEWALKS

of the glacier, however, has been almost continuous each summer since those measurements were taken. The ice cliffs that are visible on the eastern margins of Snow Dome and Mount Kitchener as you drive north from Athabasca Glacier toward Jasper are approximately 100 to 150 metres thick.

5. What does "Athabasca" mean?

The word comes from the Cree indigenous language and means "place where the reeds grow." The name refers to the Athabasca River in the area of Lake Athabasca in northeastern Alberta. Meltwater from Athabasca Glacier creates the Sunwapta River, which joins the Athabasca River not far downstream. The Athabasca River also has its origins in the Columbia Icefield, but Columbia Glacier, from which it originates, is not visible from the Icefields Parkway.

6. Is it safe to go out on the ice?

Unless you are an experienced and well-equipped mountaineer, it is dangerous to go out onto the ice on your own. One of the reasons the "Ice Explorer" excursion on Athabasca Glacier is so popular is that it ensures that everyone – no matter how inexperienced – can be safe while still having the opportunity to walk on the icy surface of a major glacier flowing down from the Columbia Icefield. For those who are more adventurous or desire a more prolonged ice-age experience, private and regularly scheduled guided walks on the ice are offered all summer long by Athabasca Glacier Icewalks.

7. Why is the ice blue?

Glacial ice is little more than compressed snow. At the centre of every snowflake is a nucleus of dust. Because of the size of the dust particles and the

nature of the crystalline structures in which they are trapped, glacial ice reflects the shorter blue and green waves of sunlight.

8. Does anything grow in or on the ice?

Yes, life can flourish but only on the snow that blankets the ice each winter. In spring and early summer, late-lying bands of winter snow often turn pink. Hikers walking on this snow often leave red footprints. This coloration is caused by a blue-green algae of the species *Chlamydomonas nivalis,* which flourishes in high-altitude snowpacks. The microscopic cells of this algae are encased in a red, gelatinous sheath which is capable of withstanding cold temperatures. This coating also protects the algae from the fierce radiation that falls on late-lying snow at altitude. Some say this snow, if eaten, has a faint taste of watermelon. Many insects can also be found living out various stages of their lives in or on the snow. Tiny ice worms are sometimes found in meltwater that pools in glacial depressions in some areas of the Rockies, but they are not common here.

9. Can you drink the water?

The water created by the melting of glacier ice can be almost as pure as distilled water. The clear glacier water that flows over the surface of Athabasca Glacier is as fresh and clean and refreshing as any water on Earth. When glacial meltwater picks up a great deal of rock flour and other fine debris, as it does at the terminus of the glacier, its colour can change to grey or brown. Though the water is still fresh, these sediments can bother sensitive stomachs if the water is consumed in large quantities over a prolonged period of time.

10. What is this area like in the winter?

Because of a gap in the mountain ranges to the west which separate the Rockies from the Pacific coast, the Columbia Icefield receives a great deal more snow than any of the regions immediately around it. An average snow year would see 10 metres of snow fall on Athabasca Glacier. It can also be windy and very cold in this part of Jasper National Park. While winter temperatures have moderated slightly in the Canadian Rockies in the early 21st century, winter temperatures of −40°C are still not uncommon.

Athabasca Glacier is a
cold and very windy place
in winter.

Water and What It Becomes in Winter

How fortunate we are to live on a planet so appropriately composed of just the right substances, enveloped in just the right atmosphere and located just the right distance from the sun to permit an abundance of water on its surface. Water is not only the stuff that composes most of the living tissue of life, it is the universal solvent in which all life's nutrients dissolve and are distributed to even the most minute chains of being on Earth. Life is an intelligent idea carried around in the mind of water. Life could even be viewed as water's way of transporting itself around. Where water goes, life follows. Life is water, and so is the earth. More than two-thirds of the world's surface is water. The atmosphere is an engine that circulates water. Not only does water define the boundaries of life on Earth, it also fashions the texture and nature of this planet's surface. Water is the earth's most enduring agent of natural change. It is a mass transporter of the elements that compose the earth. The planet, at least as life views it, is almost entirely defined by the meanderings of rivers, the reliability and distribution of annual rains and the frequency and duration of snowfall. This is water as liquid. The impact of water as snow and ice can also be immense. It is in these frozen forms that water is most visible and least subtle in its impact on the earth's crust. It is with water as snow and ice that our inquiry into the Columbia Icefield must begin.

Examining the nature of glacial ice on the surface of Athabasca Glacier. PHOTO COURTESY OF ATHABASCA GLACIER ICEWALKS

Everywhere in the polar and temperate regions, but also at high altitudes in the tropics, atmospheric water condenses and freezes into solid form. Sometimes the resulting water falls as hail or as small irregular globes called graupel. But most often, frozen atmospheric water falls as snow. Every child has marvelled at the lacy elegance inherent in the radial symmetry of the snowflake. Each flake is different, each unique, each perfect in its own way. When snow falls in the Rockies, individual flakes fall one upon the other, glistening and gradually deepening into the romantic image of the Canadian winter. As snow continues to fall and deepen, the sheer weight of accumulation changes the nature of the flakes. As pressure builds, the lovely radial arms, outstretched and intertwined, break off. Eventually the aging flakes devolve into a form of granular snow called hoar. In most places in the world, the life of hoar snow is terminated by the hot sun of springtime. The aging snow dies back into water as it melts. But at the poles, and in the high places of the earth's mountains, the snow that falls in winter doesn't always melt. Some of it remains on the ice at the end of summer, and at a given depth, perhaps 30 metres or so, the compressed snow slowly becomes ice.

This is not the thin, ephemeral ice we put in our drinks or worry about when driving, however. This is ice crystallized under the pressure of deep time. It is the ice of eternity. Under its own weight amid the force of gravity, and in response to the dictates of its crystalline nature, this ice moves. This is the ice of the eons; this is glacier ice.

How is a glacier formed?

Glaciers form in places where more snow accumulates annually than melts. The snow that does not melt away in summer but instead accumulates is known as firn snow. The density of the firn snow at the surface is around 350 kilograms per cubic metre. Over time the firn is compacted by the weight of the overlying layers and as a result of water vapour diffusion. From the surface and until a density of about 550 kg/m³ is reached, the transformation of snow to ice is dominated by increasing pressure from above which results in the rearrangement of the firn grains into a denser pack. But deeper in the snowpack, simple reorientation of the grains does not lead to significant density increase. Rather, at these depths and densities, the most important transformational processes involve coalescence of the ice mass into a solid yet plastic condition. When a density of about 800 kg/m³ is reached, the open pores filled with air that remain in the compressing ice are gradually pinched off and form bubbles in the ice. This zone is called the firn–ice transition and it spans about the bottom 10 per cent of the total firn column. Depending on temperature and the amount of snowfall, the firn zone can be between 50 and 150 metres thick, and the age of the ice can range from a few hundred years as in southern Greenland to several thousand years as in central Antarctica.

DIFFERENT TYPES OF GLACIERS

The World Glacier Monitoring Service estimates there are approximately 160,000 glaciers in the world, covering an estimated 685,000 square kilometres. Depending on latitude, altitude, topography, climate and orientation to the sun, glaciers will take a number of different forms.

Ice sheets

A body of glacial ice is considered to be an ice sheet if it assumes continental dimensions. To be an ice sheet a body of ice and snow has to be larger than 50,000 square kilometres (19,305 square miles) in area. While the northern hemisphere was once covered by them, true ice sheets are now found only in Antarctica and Greenland.

Ice streams

Ice streams are long, ribbon-like glaciers that flow within the confines of an ice sheet. Bordered by more slowly moving ice rather than mountains, these huge glacial masses can be very sensitive to the rate of loss at their termini, especially if they terminate in the ocean.

*Above: The Greenland **Ice Sheet**.*

*Right: These **ice streams** flow through the southern part of the Greenland Ice Sheet.*

Ice caps

Ice caps are smaller versions of ice sheets. Covering less than 50,000 square kilometres, ice caps form primarily in polar and sub-polar regions that are relatively flat. Ice caps are found in northern Canada and throughout the circumpolar North.

Icefields

Icefields are similar to ice caps, except that their flow is influenced by the underlying topography. Icefields are also generally smaller than ice caps.

*Sólheimajökull Glacier flows from the Mýrdalsjökull **ice cap** in southern Iceland, which covers the Katla volcano, one of the most active in Iceland. The Sólheimajökull measures about 15 km long by 1–2 km wide, covering some 44 km². The glacier terminates only 100 m above sea level.*

The degree of influence of the underlying topography that distinguishes an icefield from an ice cap is clearly apparent in this photograph of the Eyjafjallajökull **Icefield** in Iceland.

A **mountain glacier** descending from the Columbia Icefield.

Mountain glaciers

A mountain glacier is a body of ice that flows out of an icefield that spans several peaks. The Columbia Icefield is the source of three large mountain glaciers and many smaller ones.

Valley glaciers

Commonly originating from icefields in mountainous regions, valley glaciers form long tongues of ice that flow downvalley, often beyond the summer snowline, where they are subject to annual melt.

*Like the Athabasca, the Saskatchewan Glacier is a classic **valley glacier.***

Tidewater glaciers

Tidewater glaciers are valley glaciers that terminate in the ocean. Instead of melting as they might do on land, tidewater glaciers calve into icebergs which, if they drift into shipping lanes, can create serious hazards.

Hanging glaciers

As valley glaciers thin and recede, remnants of them are sometimes left in small, high valleys above the main valley into which

*While **tidewater glaciers** exist in Antarctica and Greenland, some of the most spectacular and accessible examples are found along the coast of Alaska.*

*Angel Glacier on Mount Edith Cavell north of the Columbia Icefield in Jasper National Park is a classic, accessible example of a **hanging glacier**.*

the glacier once flowed. These are called hanging glaciers. When hanging glaciers disappear, the valleys they leave behind are called hanging valleys.

Cirque glaciers

Cirques are bowls carved out of the sides of mountains by the action of glacial ice. Glaciers that create and occupy these bowls are called cirque glaciers. Such glaciers persist because they exist most commonly on high, north-facing mountainsides and thus are protected from summer heat. It is anticipated that if current warming trends continue, cirque glaciers may be among the last to survive in the Canadian Rocky Mountains.

Rock glaciers

When frost-shattered rock accumulates in cold conditions, melted snow and rain can freeze beneath the rubble, lubricating the movement of such slopes in a way that very much resembles the movement of glacial ice itself.

Above, left: The glaciers on the front side of Mount Athabasca are **cirque glaciers**.

Above, right: Though many visitors do not see what it is because of its enormous scale, there is a classic example of a **rock glacier** *that is very visible from the Icefields Parkway. It is located on one of the outliers of Mount Athabasca near Parker Ridge, just south of the Columbia Icefield.*

The Snows of Yesteryear: The Natural History of Glaciers

Glacier ice is a relatively recent phenomenon on Earth. Certainly ice could not have existed while hot swirls of cosmic gases were still condensing into the fiery turbulence of the forming Earth. Ice likely didn't exist while the still erupting surface of the earth's crust cooled into a shattered shell. Nor could it have appeared during the long, warm morning of the earth's first oceans during which proto-continents began their tireless drift over the surface of the world. Ice likely couldn't have appeared until after a relatively stable atmosphere began to cling to a more slowly turning Earth, until the planet was protected sufficiently that it was no longer being scorched by the nuclear fires of the sun. Ice likely first appeared as soon as the aura of air around this blue globe at last glowed with enough substance to be effective as an atmosphere. Still, that was a long, long time ago.

The earliest evidence of the presence of glaciers in the world appears in the middle Precambrian, amidst rock of an antiquity so distant in time that it is difficult for the mind to grasp. In North America, Africa and Australia, glacial deposits called tillites were laid down as early as 2.3 billion years ago, long before life rose

Columbia Glacier.

from the warm broth of the sea to conquer the land. In the upper Precambrian, glacial evidence presents itself again at intervals of 900, 750 and 600 million years ago, the latter evidence coinciding with some of the earliest preserved fossil life on this planet. Substantial evidence of glaciation presents itself again in the late Ordivician, during the age of the first fishes. Evidence appears again 300 million years ago, straddling the ages of the great coal-producing forests of the Permian and Carboniferous. There is a long break in the glacial record during the Triassic, Jurassic and Cretaceous. Then there is the overwhelming evidence of the stupendous Cenozoic glaciations that shaped, and continue to shape, the world as we know it today.

Though much is known about the dynamics of glacier ice, there are few questions in all of modern geology as difficult to answer as those related to why ice ages occur on Earth. There are many theories. Many factors, individually or collectively, affect where snow falls, how long it accumulates, the size and nature of accumulated glacial masses, the ability of glaciers to sustain conditions that spawn them and the changes in climate that bring ice ages to an end. Some of these theories imply the possibility of cosmic or galactic influences in the initiations of ice ages. Some theories speculate on wholesale changes in the orbit of the earth and variations in the heat output of the sun. Others speculate about planetary collisions with comet nuclei, the sun-screening effect of airborne, iridium-laced ash, the presence of visiting suns. More earthbound theories include variations in the thermal characteristics of the oceans, the effects of volcanism on the atmosphere, changes in the heat reflectivity of the earth's surface. One quite plausible theory offers that changes in the latitudes of the earth's roving continents would induce glaciation.

One of the most clearly accepted theories of glacial origins is the observation that continental uplift resulting in mountain building can elevate landmasses to the point where they force moisture-laden winds into the thinner atmosphere and colder climes of the high peaks. Under cold conditions, high moisture condenses into high snowfall, which fails to melt during the brief high-altitude summers. The eternal snows linger in basins between the high peaks. Soon the accumulated snow is compressed by its own accumulating weight into glacial ice. The ice, by its very nature, then begins to flow downhill, in the direction of least resistance, into neighbouring valleys. In the warmer climate of the lower valleys, the centuries-old ice then melts to form rivers. Though other influences may combine to create larger continental glaciations, the Columbia Icefield clearly owes its continued existence to the high-altitude ring of mountains that surround it and to the moisture-rich winds that blow inland from the Pacific to dump snow on the peaks of the Great Divide. There are no other simple ways to explain the survival of such a large ice mass so far south at this particular time in the earth's geological history.

The theory of mountain building as it relates to the Columbia Icefield has another advantage. It may be the only simple way by which the astonishing fact of this stupendous sea of ice and snow can be compressed into a concept an overwhelmed witness can readily grasp.

Ice flows toward the surrounding valleys from the great bowl of snow that is the Columbia Icefield névé. The peak dominating the background skyline is Mount Columbia.

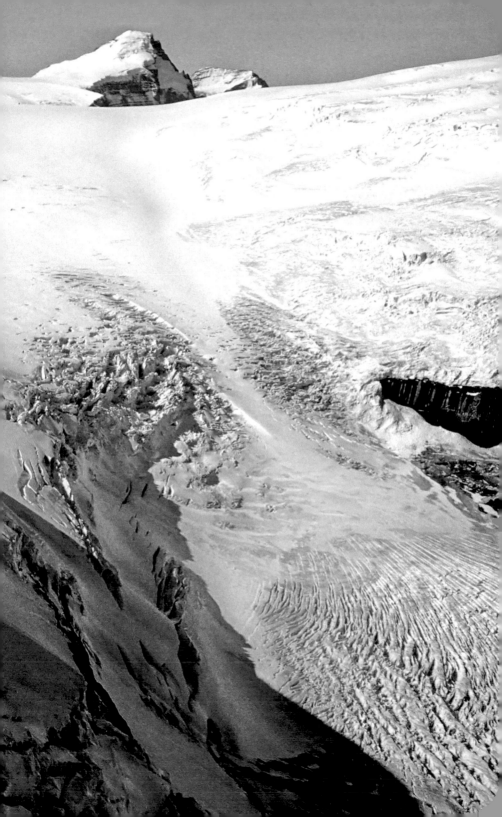

Ice ages: The ice man cometh

Though it is a bold statement without complete evidence in support, it is generally assumed that as long as there has been ice in the polar regions of this continent, glaciers have likely existed in the Canadian Rockies. While local altitude and climatic conditions may have supported glaciers in the Columbia Icefield area for as long as three million years, ice movement at the Columbia has also been linked to more widespread climatic coolings that have resulted in major glacial advances throughout the Rockies. What appears to be the most extensive of all modern ice ages appears to have begun roughly 240,000 years ago. The Illinoian, or Great Glaciation, covered most of the northern regions of the earth's upper hemisphere, fashioning much of the geography as we know it today in North America. The Great Glaciation was a spectacular geological event that lasted 100,000 years. Though the glaciers of the Columbia Icefield would have grown dramatically during this continental cooling, the dynamics of the icefield itself would have changed little. Warm, moist winds from the Pacific would deposit heavy snows along the divide between what is now British Columbia and Alberta; the snow would accumulate and compress into ice; and the ice would begin to flow down valleys already created by ancient rivers. The only difference would be that the major alpine glaciers could have been hundreds of kilometres long and as much as 2 kilometres deep as they left the Rockies and joined the even greater ice masses flowing southward from the direction of the pole.

Other notable but lesser glacial advances took place in the Rockies 75,000 and 20,000 years ago and did much to give these mountains the contours that make them so dramatic today. Another climatic cooling took place around 11,000 years ago and initiated what is called the Crowfoot Advance, a smaller but nevertheless measurable glacial growth period still represented in the surface geology of the Columbia Icefield area. The last glacial advance to have taken place in the Canadian Rockies is so recent that early travellers were able to document its close. The Cavell Advance likely began about 1200 CE, roughly around the time King Richard the Lion Heart was killed in France and the Fourth Crusade was making life miserable in Constantinople. Three subsequent phases of the Cavell Advance were dated through tree-ring analysis conducted by Dr. Brian Luckman. The maximum glacier extent appears to have occurred in the mid-18th century. Research indicates that subsequent glacier surges occurred around 1800, 1816 and later in the 19th century. At the peak of the Cavell Advance, in about 1750, Athabasca Glacier was 2 kilometres longer than it is now. Most of the other major glaciers that flow from the Columbia Icefield must have been much larger then too.

Because of the work of renowned scientists like Dr. Luckman we have a foundation for understanding what is happening in our mountains, but even our best researchers would be the first to say we don't know enough. The Canadian Rockies have experienced a 1.5°C increase in mean annual temperature over the last 100 years. During this time, increases in winter temperatures have been more than twice as large as the increases in spring and summer. The annual temperature record in the Canadian Rockies is dominated by winter conditions, which show the largest inter-annual range, 12.7°C, and the great-

Lord of the Rings, Dr. Brian Luckman.

est warming trend, 3.4°C, over the past century. In spring and summer, both numbers are more modest, with inter-annual variation of only 4 to 5°C and a warming trend of only 1.3°C over the last century. From tree-ring chronologies from a site near Athabasca Glacier at the Columbia Icefield, Dr. Luckman was able to demonstrate that summer temperatures were below late-20th-century levels from about 1100 until 1800 CE, and that the coldest summer conditions occurred during the Cavell Advance in the 19th century, which averaged 1.05°C below the 1961–1990 mean. Over the past century, the area of glacial cover in the Rockies has decreased by at least 25 per cent and glaciers have receded in length to approximately where they likely were some 3,000 years ago, before the Cavell Advance.

The Birthplace of Western Rivers

The organizing principle of the Canadian Rocky Mountain Parks World Heritage Site is watershed. The spine of the Rockies is the birthplace of western rivers. Every aspect of the mountain landscape encompassed in this World Heritage Site is an expression of what water is and does on the landscape. All of the rest of the wonder – the shapes of the peaks, the colour of the lakes, the rich forest and alpine ecosystems – all flow from the fact of abundant water. To see the World Heritage Site in this context is to understand its significance, not just to the West but to the world.

Before it is anything else, the spine of the Rockies is a hydrological feature of continental importance. Before we perceive it as home or as a tourism attraction it should be viewed first as a region of annually generated snowpack and rainfall that provides water to almost the entire West.

Everything starts at the apex of the world, which in the Canadian Rockies means the Columbia Icefield. It is from this high basin of stone and snow that the plenty

The triple hydrological apex: Jasper National Park superintendent Ron Hooper along with the author and Jasper mayor Dick Ireland send water to three great oceans from the summit of Snow Dome in celebration of the United Nations International Year of Fresh Water in 2003. PHOTO | WARD CAMERON

that is the West flows downstream to enrich the rest of the continent. If we truly want to understand this place, we have to realize that at its very foundation the Rockies are all about slopes and divides. The Rockies are all about water. With this in mind, one way to recontextualize the Canadian Rocky Mountain Parks World Heritage Site as a biophysical and cultural unit is to examine the seven magnificent parks that comprise it in the context of watershed.

Snow Dome: a triple-triple divide

Beyond the experience of the utterly monumental in nature, even a brief visit to the Columbia Icefield teaches us that water is a central element in determining what the surface of the earth was like at any given moment in its history. A change of only a few degrees in atmospheric temperature will govern what forms water will take and how it will act in shaping the world and the life forms that exist in it at any moment in Earth time. Of all the extraordinary glacial features offering testimony to the importance of water in making the world that exists at the Columbia Icefield, Snow Dome is perhaps the most amazing, for it is a triple continental divide.

A divide is the boundary between the headwaters of a drainage basin. In lowlands – especially where the ground is marshy – drainage divides may be hard to discern. Lower drainage divides on valley floors are often defined by deposition or stream capture. In mountainous regions, divides usually lie along topographical ridges, which often take the form of a single range of hills or mountains. Since ridgelines are easy to see, drainage divides are natural borders that are often used to define

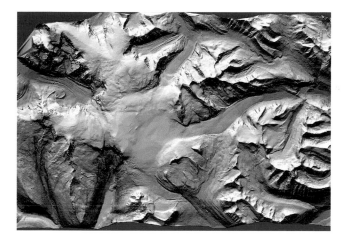

A digital elevation model illustrating the dimensions of the Columbia Icefield in 1949. IMAGE COURTESY OF THE GLACIOLOGY SECTION OF THE GEOLOGICAL SURVEY OF CANADA

political boundaries such as that between Alberta and British Columbia.

A continental divide is the boundary between watersheds that flow into different oceans. A triple continental divide is rare in nature. It is the uppermost point that separates water that flows in different directions across a continent to pour ultimately into not two but three separate oceans. The apex of the triple continental divide at the Columbia Icefield is the summit of Snow Dome, a 3510-metre peak that overlooks Athabasca Glacier from the north. Depending on where snow falls at the summit of this mountain, it can, upon melting, end up in any one of three major river systems, each bound for a different ocean. From the gently dipping northern shoulder of the mountain, melt joins the waters of the Athabasca River, which flow nearly 3000 kilometres

After leaving Jasper National Park, the Athabasca River flows northeast into Lake Athabasca, the waters of which flow northward to create the Mackenzie River system.

northward through the massive Mackenzie River system to become part of the Arctic Ocean. Meltwaters from the mountain's western shoulder flow through the Bush and Wood rivers into the Columbia, which meanders 2000 kilometres southwestward to join the Pacific near Portland, Oregon. From Snow Dome's eastern shoulders, the flow is into the North Saskatchewan, the great stream of the northern Canadian plains, coursing nearly 2000 kilometres to join Atlantic tidewater at Hudson Bay.

While Snow Dome was viewed initially as a worthy mountaineering objective and then as an interesting hydrological feature, it has come to stand for a great deal more. As our scientific awareness grows, we now understand the importance of the Columbia Icefield as a climatic thermostat and water tower for western North

America. If you are among those who believe that life itself has the collective capacity to self-regulate the surface temperatures of Earth to create optimal conditions for sustained biodiversity, you will be interested to know that Snow Dome also represents "the triple point of water." The term refers to the temperature range at which all three phases of water – solid, liquid and vapour – coexist and interact. This range, between –40 and +40°C, is absolutely crucial to tolerable climate variability and to life processes, and at its centre is the freezing point of water. Looking up at the lip of ice visible from the Icefields Parkway, one gets a sense of what this means to the landscape and to those who live there. Our entire existence is clustered around the triple point of water.

The triple continental divide on Snow Dome is unique also in that it is so deeply blanketed in glacial ice. Over the last three decades the glaciers of the mountain West have been shrinking faster than at any other time in recorded history. If the world continues to warm and all this "water in the bank" disappears, the West, and our entire continent, will be a very different place.

In this larger context, Snow Dome could be seen as a *triple*-triple divide: it performs its basic function of separating mountain meltwaters to send them on their respective ways to three different oceans; it reflects the atmospheric temperature balance that determines the proportion of water that exists on the planet in each of its various and highly active forms; and third, it functions as a baseline, dividing past hydrological regimes from those of the present and those that will exist in the future, not just in the Rockies but in the entire West.

A visual tour of the Columbia Icefield

A counter-clockwise trip around the Columbia Icefield, starting at Athabasca Glacier, moving north over Dome Glacier to Snow Dome, to Columbia Glacier and Mount Columbia and then south over Castleguard Glacier, the enormous Saskatchewan Glacier, up the Big Hill to Mount Athabasca and back to Athabasca Glacier and the Columbia Icefield Visitor Centre.

Athabasca Glacier in October. The katabatic winds that spill down the glacier from the Columbia Icefield have removed all of the previous winter's snow and polished the ice.

Above: Stepping back from the terminus of Athabasca Glacier, it is possible to see its proximity to adjacent Dome Glacier, which pours down from the upper reaches of the Columbia Icefield.

Left: Dome Glacier spilling down from the shoulders of Snow Dome. Much of its ice is covered by moraines.

53

Top: Stutfield Glacier, named for Hugh Stutfield, a British mountaineer who accompanied Norman Collie on the 1898 expedition northward from Lake Louise during which the Columbia Icefield was discovered.

Bottom: The triple continental divide on Snow Dome is a remarkable feature, one that would alone have qualified the Canadian Rocky Mountain Parks for consideration as a World Heritage Site.

Top: The upper snows of the Columbia Icefield.

Bottom: At 3747 m, Mount Columbia is the highest peak in the Columbia Icefield group and in Alberta.

Columbia Glacier, which flows
from the northern rim of the
Columbia Icefield, forms the
headwaters of the Athabasca
River, a major western Canadian
watercourse.

Above: Mount Castleguard, with Mount Columbia in the background.

Left: Rivers of meltwater course down Saskatchewan Glacier during peak summer thaw.

Left: Saskatchewan Glacier and the Big Loop on the Icefields Parkway, just below the big hill up the south side of Sunwapta Pass. This glacier is about 6 km from the parkway, over extremely rough terrain. Because of the changing nature of the glacier's terminus, this route is recommended for experienced climbers only.

Below: Mount Athabasca is one of the principal geological features of the Columbia Icefield region. Besides cradling Athabasca Glacier on its northern shoulder, this 3491-m peak also has its own spectacular glaciers as shown here.

Athabasca Glacier in late summer when the past winter's snow has melted, exposing the full grandeur of its three headwall icefalls and the entire extent of ice not covered by lateral moraines.

How do icefields produce their own weather?

It seems obvious that air is going to be cooled if it passes over a 220-square-kilometre block of snow-covered ice, but an icefield can affect more than just the air directly above it. If you visit the Columbia Icefield, you may notice a cold breeze coming from the direction of whatever glacier you are looking at. The cold breeze is caused by the same force of nature that makes rocks roll downhill – gravity. Cold air is denser than warm air, and thus heavier. As the air passing over the icefield cools, gravity pulls it downhill and you experience what is called a katabatic wind.

As the images below demonstrate, glaciers, by their very presence, also have a direct and lasting refrigerating effect on immediate and surrounding landscapes. In the visible-light images below we see the reflectivity of the ice at the terminus of Athabasca Glacier.

In autumn, when the temperature gradient between the icefield and the lower valleys is greatest, katabatic winds can be powerful enough to literally polish the surface of the glacier.

The thermal image of the same terminus at the exact same time demonstrates just how much colder the ice is compared to the surrounding landscape. The thermal image also shows just how warm the dark-coloured rocks that form Athabasca Glacier's terminal moraines can become in midsummer.

Because it takes 79 times more heat to raise the temperature of ice than it does to raise the temperature of liquid water, it has been estimated that the loss of Northern sea ice will cause as much warming as can be attributed to 70 per cent of the CO_2 presently in the earth's atmosphere.

These glaciers help refrigerate the world. A great many mountains that were once covered in snow and ice are already darkening and drying. Such mountains reflect less light and retain more heat.

The visible-light photographs are by R.W. Sandford. The infrared image of the same glacier was made simultaneously by Dr. John Pomeroy of the Centre for Hydrology at the University of Saskatchewan.

Often, as a consequence, the ice that is holding them together disappears. If our mountain glaciers disappear, the heat presently withdrawn from the atmosphere to melt glacial ice will suddenly be available to further heat the atmosphere. The result will be greater instability. We are already observing this trend in many of the world's high mountain ranges.

Moulin bleu: the glacial surface

The most telling characteristic of glacial ice is its plasticity under pressure. As snow falls and becomes ice in the icefield collecting basin, a number of things happen to it. As the snowflakes are flattened they lose their characteristic crystalline shapes. Most of the air trapped between the flakes is driven out, and once this happens the resulting ice has greater density and a different crystal structure. This ice now is under great pressure. If the ice has a place to move to in response to that pressure, it becomes a glacier.

While under pressure, glacier ice is neither a true fluid like water in its liquid form nor a true solid like stone in its cool state. Under extreme pressure, glacial ice acts in the way a plastic might, in that its molecular structure allows it to flow over itself and over obstacles that stand in its way. A glacier, especially one like the Athabasca, is most plastic at its centre, where it is under the greatest pressure from its own weight and under the least influence of drag caused by the movement of its huge mass over the highly resistant bed over which the ice haltingly flows. This plasticity quite literally gives the glacier the capacity to stretch. This capacity is limited, however. If a glacier stretches too much, it dissipates the internal pressures that gives the ice its plasticity. This often happens when the glacier flows over irregularities beneath its surface, and it gives rise to a number of beautiful but often very dangerous glacial features. When the glacier flows over particularly large irregularities, like the upper cliff that forms the headwall just below the top of Athabasca Glacier, the ice stretches to the point where its depth and plasticity are not enough to allow it to bridge the obstruction. The ice then fractures and breaks into towers of broken ice called

Athabasca Glacier from above the headwall, looking down toward the Icefields Visitor Centre.

séracs. As the glacier pushes each of these towers over the cliff edge, they collect at the bottom and immediately reconstitute themselves under the pressure of their own weight into plastic glacier ice that resumes its journey toward the toe. Where the irregularity over which the glacier flows is smaller in relation to the depth of the glacier, the stretching of the ice causes crevasses to form.

A photo tour of glacier surface features

When glacial ice flows down a very steep wall it can form pressure ridges called ogives. The ogives on Columbia Glacier show textbook uniformity and add to the stunning beauty of this remote glacier as it flows from the Columbia Icefield to become the headwaters of the Athabasca River.

Top: Séracs at the icefalls at the headwall of Athabasca Glacier.

Bottom: Meltwater streams on the surface of Athabasca Glacier.

The spring melt cleanses the glacier surface of almost everything that fell with – or was under – the snow during the winter. Not all of that debris will be washed away, however, and more will join it as the summer progresses. As the melt continues, slivers of rock eroded from surrounding mountains mix with particulate matter that fell with the snow such as pollen, insect wings and burnt pine needles. Not to mention tiny motes of stardust fallen from passing comets or asteroids in space or micro-fragments of the Great Wall of China blown in on winds from Asia. During the spring and summer melt, all this various material collects into unearthly-looking, dark-coloured pyramids called cryoconite piles.

Top: Serpentine stream flows on Athabasca Glacier.

Bottom: At nearly 10 km in length, the Saskatchewan is the largest glacier flowing from the Columbia Icefield. This glacier forms the headwaters of the North Saskatchewan River. The dark line down the right side is a medial moraine, a common lateral moraine created when two glaciers meet and join. The slopes on the right are part of Parker Ridge, one of the best vantage points from which to observe Saskatchewan Glacier.

As we see in this photo of Castleguard Glacier, the firn line separating the bare ice exposed in summer from the lingering winter snows is not always straight. Only after the winter's snow is gone do the more spectacular surface features of the glacier become the most visible.

On warm summer days, surface flows on Athabasca Glacier can be substantial. The streaming water polishes the ice, creating very slippery conditions for those walking on the glacier without crampons.

Glacial striations are marks left on the rock surface below a glacier as the ice grinds gravel and debris over the rock as it advances. As evidenced by the marks on the bedrock left behind on this unnamed glacier on the west side of the Columbia Icefield, glacial striations are well exposed as glaciers recede.

Athabasca Glacier Icewalks guide Bernard Faure stands on similar glacial striations at the terminus of Athabasca Glacier.

An ice cave on Athabasca Glacier. PHOTO COURTESY OF ATHABASCA GLACIER ICEWALKS

A millwell on the Athabasca Glacier.

A survivor's tale: A story of inexperience, incompetence and extraordinarily good luck

The story is still told to disbelieving tourists. Imagine this. A man actually disappeared beneath the ice and was washed through the glacier to come out its snout. It sounds like just another bus-driver tall tale but it is nevertheless true.

It all began innocently enough. After viewing a dizzying array of mountain-climbing photographs projected on the wall by a friend, I decided I wanted to become a mountaineer. No point in half measures. The first backpacking trip I did in my entire life was across the Columbia Icefield. I only had two days off work, but that, in my opinion, ought to have been enough. After all, when you are 20 years old, how big can an icefield be?

The accident happened while we were descending Saskatchewan Glacier on the afternoon of the second day. I was so tired that I had given up even trying to avoid the big meltwater streams coursing across the glacier's broken surface. I was cold and wet and worn out and all I wanted to do was get down. So I took a shortcut.

Unless you have travelled on a big glacier, it is hard to imagine how much melt can occur on a hot day. There are actually rivers on the surface of the ice. Seeking a direct line, I tried to cross one.

The power of the icy water lifted me up and carried me to the mouth of a huge crevasse. One moment I was looking at the sun sparkle of splashing water; a moment later I was in the centre of a waterfall plunging into complete darkness beneath the ice. The waterfall cascaded down a series of ice lips to join the river that flowed beneath the glacier. Never before or since have I heard from everywhere around me so many of the different sounds that water makes. Here I was inside a planetary artery, examining first-hand what water does to the world. But then I had this little problem. Only a few inches separated the top of the water and the roof of the ice. In darkness, I kept smashing into boulders and scraping against the underside of the glacier. But just as the shock and

The Saskatchewan Glacier and its outwash plain.

wonder were beginning to evaporate, just as calm was about to become sheer terror, the strangest thing happened. The ice above began to glow. At first it was a faint green. As the river swept me onward the glow intensified. Green gradually merged into a pale blue. I noticed then that rocks were hanging out of a ceiling made entirely of light. Then I washed out of the glacier into sunshine and into the full flood of the North Saskatchewan River, where my problems really began.

The accident changed everything. My life flowed toward unexpected ends. I realize now that I have spent the rest of my life trying to prevent my own culture from carrying me permanently downstream and away from the luminous glory of that subglacial light. This book is a testament to how much that experience shaped my identity and how important the Columbia Icefield remains in the life and work of so many who care about the remarkable character of Canada's mountain West.

The moraines of Athabasca Glacier as they looked in 2008.

The aerial photograph of Athabasca Glacier opposite dramatically reveals the effects that millions of tonnes of moving ice can have on the landscape beneath. The first thing that is obvious is the effect of the moving ice on the shape of the valley. Valleys carved by rivers are V-shaped, while valleys accentuated by the mass movement of glacial ice are U-shaped. This effect on the contours of mountain valleys can be observed all along the Icefields Parkway.

The next depositional features that are very obvious are the lateral moraines, the steep, knife-shaped piles of broken rock that the moving ice pushes up on either side of the glacier. Some of these moraines are nearly a hundred metres high, evidence of the fact that the glacier was recently much longer and deeper than it is today. The knife shape of these moraines is very clear at the bottom left of the photograph, where we can see the road taken by buses to where the Ice Explorer tour used to begin at the time this picture was taken. These later moraines collapse over the ice and may remain ice-cored long after the main body of the glacier has disappeared. In a warming climate, however, the ice buried beneath lateral moraines eventually melts, making such roads impossible to maintain for long, which is why the starting point of the Ice Explorer tour continu-ally changes. The lateral moraines on the Athabasca have become

so unstable that it may eventually be necessary for the Ice Explorer tour to get onto the ice by way of the toe of the glacier in the same way Alex Watt did when he began offering tours using half-tracks in 1948.

Above: Another classic surface feature is the medial moraine, a common formation where two glacial sources converge. From a distance the medial moraine on Saskatchewan Glacier looks like a highway. Up close, however, you see that it is hardly a highway at all, but instead is a jumble of broken rock and smaller debris called scree.

An Ice Explorer climbing the steep lateral moraine of Athabasca Glacier. The tour operator quite correctly explains that the road onto the glacier from the passenger transfer station on the moraine is touted as one of the steepest commercial roads to have ever existed in Canada, making access to the ice part of the thrill of the experience.

Terminal moraines are another large-scale depositional feature that can be readily seen at Athabasca Glacier. These moraines are formed as the constantly moving ice deposits rocks, gravel and fine

dust called rock flour at the snout of the glacier. Terminal moraines can become quite large if the glacier stays in the same place, which only happens when the amount of summer melt does not exceed winter advance. Athabasca Glacier, however, is retreating, which means the terminal moraine is receding along the margin of the ice.

Another feature typical of glacial landscapes is the proglacial lake. These are lakes that form at the very terminus of a melting glacier. These are often impermanent features that come and go depending on the amount of debris deposited in them by meltwater. At the time of this writing a proglacial lake – which locals call Sunwapta Lake – existed at the terminus of Athabasca Glacier. The best example of a proglacial lake in the Columbia Icefield, however, is the as yet unnamed lake shown here, which has formed at the terminus of Columbia Glacier.

In some places, proglacial lakes can become quite large and relatively permanent. In such circumstances much of the sediment deposited in the lake by the melting ice can settle, leaving only fine dust particles, called rock flour, suspended in the water. These particles are of just the right size to reflect back the blue spectrum of sunlight, resulting in the spectacular turquoise colour of many of the famous lakes in the Canadian Rockies, including Lake Louise, Peyto Lake and Bow Lake (pictured here) in Banff National Park, as well as Maligne Lake in Jasper National Park.

Glacier meltwaters carry huge loads of sediment great distances downstream. Where the landscape flattens out, these sediments are deposited on what are called outwash plains. Braided streams are formed as the water finds its way around the sediments it has deposited. Pictured here is the outwash plain of the Alexandra River, just south of the Columbia Icefield. The Icefields Parkway skirts this outwash plain at a place called Graveyard Flats.

Vantage: Parker Ridge

A popular way to explore the Columbia Icefield is to take the 3-kilometre trail up the rolling shoulders of Parker Ridge. This beautiful ridge is named for well-known American climber Herschel Parker, who visited the Columbia Icefield with Walter Wilcox in 1896. The wide trail up the ridge wanders through old firs and Engelmann spruce at the edge of timberline and into the open alpine. In summer it is a natural rock garden, resplendent with every imaginable colour of wildflower. Before cresting the ridge, the trail also passes impressive 350- to 400-million-year-old fossil corals. Once the summit is reached, Saskatchewan Glacier and its outwash plain dominate the view. Nearly twice as long as Athabasca Glacier, the Saskatchewan flows gently from the high cold of the icefield into a deeply cut valley that falls steeply off from the view-point at the end of the trail.

The Saskatchewan Glacier from Parker Ridge.

Though this is one of the very best short hiking trails in all of the Canadian Rockies, it has been badly abused by inexperienced hikers who won't stay on the trails in springtime and by those who destroy the fragile tundra by shortcutting on their return trip down the gentle switchbacks. If you do not have footwear that will allow you to stay strictly on the trail, you really shouldn't attempt this walk. If you do have proper boots, though, and you are prepared to make a few concessions to the fragility of alpine vegetation, a journey to the top of this ridge could be a turning point in your appreciation for the icefield.

CROWFOOT GLACIER

Originating in a small icefield just above it, this hanging glacier just north of Lake Louise is plainly visible from the Icefields Parkway. It is called Crowfoot because when it was first seen by explorers it had a third toe which extended to the valley floor. Over the last century the glacier has lost that lower toe and has thinned considerably.

BOW GLACIER AND BOW LAKE

Bow Glacier has its origins in the Wapta Icefield, which is only barely visible from the Icefields Parkway. Melt from Bow Glacier forms Bow Lake, which is the headwaters of the Bow River flowing past Banff, through Calgary and onward over the Great Plains. Once it leaves Banff National Park, the Bow is one of the most important and heavily used rivers in Alberta.

PEYTO GLACIER AND THE WAPTA ICEFIELD

Peyto Glacier is the source of waters that pour into Peyto Lake, the headwaters of the Mistaya River, which in turn flows into the North Saskatchewan near Saskatchewan River Crossing on the Icefields Parkway. This glacier was the only one in the Canadian Rocky Mountain parks to be selected as a reference glacier by the World Glacier Monitoring Service. Though fed by the Wapta Icefield, Peyto Glacier has retreated to such an extent that glaciologists fear it will soon no longer exhibit the flow dynamics that define it as a glacier.

THE WAPTA ICEFIELD

Like the Columbia Icefield, the Wapta is a high, cold basin of eternal snows in which glacial ice is formed through the weight of accumulation and begins to flow in the direction of least resistance, which is usually downhill. Also like the Columbia Icefield, the Wapta straddles the Great Divide – the high ridge of mountains that separates the waters that flow to the Pacific from those that flow into the Atlantic, and which also marks the boundary between Alberta and British Columbia. A number of significant glaciers flow down both sides of the Great Divide from this icefield.

THE WAPTA ICEFIELD AND YOHO GLACIERS

Yoho Glacier is one of several that flow down the west side of the Great Divide from the Wapta and Waputik icefields. It forms the headwaters of the Yoho River, which joins the Kicking Horse on its way into the Columbia River system and is one of the most spectacular features in Yoho National Park.

SNOWBIRD GLACIER

Snowbird Glacier, visible from the Icefields Parkway near Peyto Lake in Banff National Park, is an example of both a cirque glacier and a hanging glacier. The tail and the body and wings of the "snowbird" were connected until warming conditions in 2009 resulted in the glacier breaking into two sections.

FRESHFIELD GLACIER

There are some very large glaciers in northern Banff National Park that cannot be seen from the Icefields Parkway. Among these is the spectacularly complex Freshfield Glacier, which flows from its own icefield. Freshfield releases its meltwaters into the Howse River below Howse Pass, on the fabled fur-trade route established by mapmaker David Thompson in 1807.

THE MONS ICEFIELD WEST AND SOUTH GLACIERS

Located in a remote and seldom travelled region north of Freshfield Glacier in Banff National Park, the Mons Icefield feeds a number of glaciers. These two were at one time a single glacier formed by the joining of two tongues separated by what is called a nunatak, or glacial island, which in this case is a mountain rising out of the surrounding ice. The glacier has since shrunk back into its sources and the two tongues no longer merge.

THE MONS ICEFIELD AND MONS GLACIER

The Mons icefield and glacier are located in the upper reaches of the Glacier River in northern Banff National Park. Note the very well-defined line between the surface of the glacier and where the snows from the previous winter remain unmelted. This is called the firn line, which in late summer delineates the glacier proper from the icefield that forms it.

THE LYELL ICEFIELD AND SOUTHEAST LYELL GLACIER

The Lyell Icefield can be glimpsed in the distance from a viewpoint looking west toward the Howse River valley, near Saskatchewan River Crossing on the Icefields Parkway. Melt from the steep and torturously crevassed Southeast Lyell Glacier flows into Glacier Lake, a popular destination for hikers and backpackers.

THE COLUMBIA ICEFIELD WEST SIDE GLACIERS

While the more accessible glaciers that flow down the eastern slopes of the Great Divide receive most of the attention, a great number of glaciers that originate in the Columbia Icefield also flow down the west side of the Divide into BC's Hamber Provincial Park, one of the least visited but most spectacular gems in the UNESCO Canadian Rocky Mountain Parks World Heritage Site.

CHISEL PEAK AND THE GLACIERS ABOVE FORTRESS LAKE

The high alpine regions of Hamber Provincial Park are little better known today than when they were first mapped a century ago. By saving, protecting and reconnecting every possible piece, the Canadian Rocky Mountain Parks World Heritage Site has not only reintegrated a vast temperate mountain ecosystem, but also preserved icefields and glaciers that are now known to be a vital part of the natural thermostat that has regulated the climate of the northern hemisphere for millions of years.

Signposts on the road to
the terminus of Athabasca
Glacier illustrate the
rapid rate of recession of
the Athabasca and other
Columbia Icefield glaciers
during the past century.

We live in a glass house warmed by an infinitesimal part of the energy sent out by a furnace 92,000,000 miles away. All life of plant or animal depends on the temperature of the surface of the earth and its envelopes. If we received a few degrees less heat from the sun much of the world would be uninhabitable, and the same is true if our atmosphere became a less efficient blanket against loss of heat by radiation into space. On the other hand an important increase in the sun's radiation or of the power of the atmosphere to retain it might blast all life by the rise in temperature. Comparatively slight changes in the supply of heat would disarrange our whole economy if they did not destroy life. It is evident that the question of the permanence or variability of climate is a vital one.

—Arthur Philemon Coleman,
Ice Ages, Recent and Ancient, 1926

Glaciers and Climate

The five crucial functions of snow and ice

What we are talking about when we talk about water in its frozen state is what scientists call the cryosphere: those portions of the earth's surface where water exists in the form of snow cover, glaciers, ice sheets and shelves, freshwater ice, sea ice, icebergs, permafrost and ground ice.

The cryosphere influences the global climate system in five significant ways. The first has to do with the extraordinary extent to which snow and ice reflect sunlight back into the atmosphere. This high degree of reflectivity, called albedo, operates as a climate feedback mechanism.

The expansion of surface snow and ice cover increases the albedo of Earth's surface, which lowers the temperature and thus enables ice and snow to spread even farther. On average, 23 per cent of the globe at any given time is covered by snow, and the effect of snow cover is most pronounced where the land mass is as large as it is in Canada. Mean monthly air temperature can be moderated by as much 5°C just because of the presence of snow. Over the past decade in particular, however, this effect has been working in the opposite direction.

Snow and ice cover is shrinking, reducing reflectivity and increasing the absorption of solar radiation, which in turn increases temperature and further reduces snow and ice cover.

The second major influence of the cryosphere is the thermal insulation of the land surface by snow cover and by lake and river ice. This blanketing effect greatly modifies the temperature regime on the underlying land or water. One of the qualities that makes snow such a central ecological influence is its capacity to shield living soil from the full effects of deep winter freezing. The temperature of the upper surface of a 10-centimetre-deep snowdrift may drop by more than 10°C overnight, but the underlying ground may cool by only 1°. The thermal conductivity of snow varies with its liquid water content, which is in turn affected by depth. In many circumstances the thermal conductivity of soil can be six times higher than that of the snow above it. This means that a layer of snow can insulate over six times more effectively than the equivalent depth of soil. By keeping the near surface from cooling to the same temperature as the atmosphere, snow cover keeps the roots of trees and other plants warm enough to prevent the depth of freezing that would create fatal ice-crystal formation in their cells. It is not just ecosystems that benefit from this effect. We humans do too. In many parts of Canada, the presence of deep snow is what keeps the soil warm enough to grow grain crops like winter wheat.

A third way in which the cryosphere influences the global hydrological cycle is through the storage of water in snow, glaciers, ice caps and ice sheets, together with associated delays in freshwater runoff. The time scales related to such releases range from weeks to months in the case of snow cover, from decades to centuries for glaciers; and from tens of thousands to hundreds of thousands of years for ice sheets and permafrost.

Snow is a reservoir that stores water in precisely the way a dam does, for gradual release downstream over the course of the spring and, in many mountain ranges, long into the summer. There is not enough money in the world to build all the dams that would be required to store all the water that the winter snowpack does for later release into streams and rivers. Cold provides this invaluable service for free.

Snow is also a medium of water transport. As researchers such as the University of Saskatchewan's Dr. John Pomeroy have demonstrated, snow is widely relocated by wind and intercepted by vegetation. When that snow melts it provides crucially important water to the ecosystems where it has collected.

A fourth function of the cryosphere is paradoxical to the point of being other-worldly: snow acts as a heat bank – a kind of thermal battery – which stores and releases energy over time.

Snow is stubborn and it takes a lot of heat to melt it. The amount of energy required to melt 1 kilogram of snow that is already at 0°C is equivalent to the energy it takes to raise the temperature of 1 kilogram of liquid water 79°C. This is why snow is such an effective climatic

Dr. John Pomeroy holds a Canada Research Chair in Hydrology and Climate Change at the University of Saskatchewan but conducts much of his research on snow and glacier ice in the Canadian Rockies.

refrigerant. It also takes a lot of heat to vaporize, or sublimate, snow. To turn 1 kilogram of snow directly into vapour takes roughly the amount of energy needed to raise the temperature of 10 kilograms of liquid water 67°C. You can see from this that having snow around keeps a lot of heat out of the atmosphere.

In the absence of snow the total amount of energy stored in the climate system at any given time will increase. Because snow normally blankets more than half of the land in the northern hemisphere each year, and possesses such important properties, seasonal snow cover is recognized as a defining ecological factor throughout the circumpolar world. The ongoing loss of snow's refrigerating feedback will cause land surfaces to warm and atmospheric temperatures to rise, with direct consequences for almost every ecosystem in this country.

The fifth major role the cryosphere plays in moderating the earth's climate system is through modulation of carbon exchange with the atmosphere. Seasonally frozen ground and permafrost slow the release of stored carbon dioxide and methane into the atmosphere. Permafrost is particularly important in this process. Deep permafrost can take 100,000 years to form. Once formed, it can store or cap enormous volumes of carbon, preventing its escape into the atmosphere. Once permafrost thaws, however, the carbon dioxide and methane stored within and beneath it is quickly mobilized.

Snow cover, glacier loss and water supply

Almost all of Earth's snow and ice-covered land is located in the northern hemisphere. Snow cover in the northern hemisphere ranges from about 46 million square kilometres in January to about 3.8 million in August. Almost all of the 9.9 million square kilometre extent of Canada can be covered by snow in January.

Dr. Garry Clarke on Parker Ridge, with Saskatchewan Glacier in the background. Dr. Clarke is considered by many to be the dean of Canadian glaciologists. His careful analyses and outstanding visual interpretations of the outcomes of his work have changed the way we look at the future of glaciers, not just in North America but around the world. PHOTO COURTESY OF THE WESTERN CANADIAN CRYOSPHERIC NETWORK

But in terms of water and climate, snow is one thing, glacial ice quite another. The importance of glacial ice to who we are as Canadians is difficult to exaggerate. The glaciers of past ice ages have completely shaped Canada as we know it. The recession of glaciers created this country's unparalleled system of streams and rivers. It was the scouring action of glacier ice that created most of our two million lakes. The melting of glacier ice created the greatest freshwater feature on the entire planet – the Great Lakes. The rebounding of the continent from the great weight of the continental ice sheets continues to fashion our geography and the patterns of Canadian settlement. And perhaps most important, the remnants of the last ice age continue to shape our climate and our weather; they define our watersheds and contribute significantly to the flow of some of our most important rivers. Fossil water frozen in time in our remaining glaciers is water in the bank for future generations of Canadians.

In most places in the world where glaciers have been studied, however, efforts have not been continuous, resulting in lengthy gaps in the data collected. Globally there are only 39 glaciers that have been studied for more than 30 years, and only 30 "reference" glaciers exist that have been subject to continuous measurement since 1976. Research conducted on the world's 30 reference glaciers indicates a cumulative global loss in glacial mass of 20 per cent in the 60 years between 1945 and 2005, which suggests that a great deal of the world's ice has already become water. Due to funding cuts to science, research in the high glaciated regions of the Rockies has been quite limited compared to what is being conducted in other mountainous places in the world. What scientists are observing in the Columbia Icefield region and throughout the mountains of the Canadian West, however, appears to be consistent with global trends.

The first estimates of glacier change in terms of area and volume for the North and South Saskatchewan river basins and the eastern slopes of the Canadian Rockies were released in a report produced by Mike Demuth of the Geological Survey of Canada and Al Pietroniro of Environment Canada's National Water Research Institute in 2004. This work was advanced further in 2006, and additional research was done by David Sauchyn and others in 2008 to predict potential glacial recession. In 2009 Laura Comeau of University of Saskatchewan confirmed the degree of loss of glacial ice in the upper regions of the Saskatchewan system, which has its origins in the Columbia Icefield.

Between 1975 and 1998, glacier cover as measured

by area decreased by approximately 22 per cent in the North Saskatchewan basin and by 36 per cent in the South Saskatchewan. Some three million people live in these two river basins. The ice volume wastage estimated for the North Saskatchewan, expressed as an annual average, is equivalent to the amount of water used by approximately 1.5 million people. When there is little or no ice left to become water, the growing needs of water-reliant populations, industries and agricultural sectors will exert ever-increasing pressure on water availability.

It has been calculated that the 1,300 glaciers on the eastern slopes of the Rockies alone supply approximately 7776 billion litres, or nearly 7.8 cubic kilometres, of water to rivers flowing into Alberta and beyond. Research on Canada's glaciers provides a clearer picture of what we can expect in terms of changing water supply as mean global temperatures continue to rise. All studies indicate that dangerously warm years like 2003 are likely to become more common. We know what extreme temperatures did to the Alps, which in places lost 10 per cent of glacial mass in only one summer. We are only now beginning to understand the impacts here. In 2003 extreme minimum-temperature increases as reported from recording stations in the Rockies were in the range of 7° to 8°C above average. The fear, of course, is that extreme temperature events of this magnitude could push our climate system out of equilibrium. The problem, as climate scientists have already indicated, is that we are not ready for these kinds of changes, which appear to be accelerating.

Athabasca Glacier in October.

According to glaciologists in the Western Canadian Cryospheric Network, Jasper National Park had 554 glaciers in 1985. Twenty years later, 135 of those had disappeared and the area of the park covered by glacial ice had been reduced by 13 per cent. In 1985, the year Banff National Park celebrated its centennial, the park had 365 glaciers within its boundaries covering 625 square kilometres. Twenty years later, 29 of those glaciers had disappeared and the area of the park covered by ice had been reduced by 19 per cent to just over 500 square kilometres.

The aggregate loss is almost staggering. In 1985 there were 1,155 glaciers in the western mountain national parks. In 2005 there were only 1,006. In other words, 149 glaciers disappeared from our western mountain national parks in only 20 years. Up until now the world's attention has been focused on the rapid loss of glacier ice in Glacier National Park in the United States, where 113 of the 150 glaciers that existed in 1860 have vanished. We now know that in Canada's mountain national parks alone, we have lost as many glaciers in only 20 years as existed a century ago in Glacier National Park. And the loss is even greater if you extend it over a longer period of time.

Through the efforts of research networks such as IP3 at the University of Saskatchewan and the Western Canadian Cryospheric Network (WC²N), we now know that we may have lost as many 300 glaciers in the Canadian Rockies between 1920 and 2005. Some 150 glaciers disappeared in the 65 years between 1920 and 1985. Another 150 disappeared into thin air in the 20 years between 1985 and 2005. Our losses appear to be accelerating.

The extent of newly deglaciated landscape is substantial. It is important to reiterate, however, that glacial ice is not just water in the bank, so to speak. As we have seen, it is also a refrigerant that moderates climate and slows climate change effects.

Because it takes 79 times more heat to raise the temperature of ice than it does to raise the temperature of liquid water, it has been estimated that the loss of northern sea ice will cause as much warming as can be attributed to 70 per cent of the CO_2 presently in the Earth's atmosphere. If our mountain glaciers disappear, the heat presently withdrawn from the atmosphere to melt glacial ice will suddenly be available to further heat the surrounding landscapes as well as the atmosphere.

These glaciers help refrigerate the world. A great many mountains that once were covered in snow and ice are already darkening in colour and drying. Such mountains reflect less light and retain more heat. Often, as a consequence, the ice that is holding them together disappears. The result is greater instability. We are already observing this trend in many of the world's high mountain ranges.

Picturing the future of the Rockies glaciers

If the warming trends witnessed since 1985 persist, the glaciers of the mountain West are on their way out. This was made abundantly clear in an animated series of climate change projections for the Canadian Rockies created by Dr. Garry Clarke of the University of British Columbia and his colleagues in the Western Canadian Cryospheric Network.

Recalculating the area of the Columbia Icefield

As part of joint research conducted by the Western Canadian Cryospheric Network, Dr. Shawn Marshall worked with Dr. Brian Menounos of the University of Northern British Columbia to accurately recalculate the current area of the Columbia Icefield. In most previous literature the icefield has been estimated at around

Dr. Clarke's time-lapse animations of what warmer temperatures could do to the remaining glaciers in the Canadian Rockies do not invite reverie. These animations will be especially troubling to people intimately familiar with the landscapes they portray.
TIME-LAPSE ILLUSTRATIONS COURTESY OF THE WESTERN CANADIAN CRYOSPHERIC NETWORK

2002

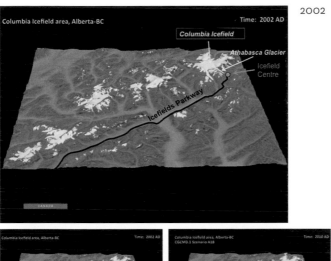

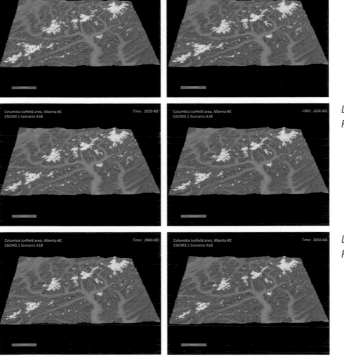

Left: 2002
Right: 2010

Left: 2020
Right: 2030

Left: 2040
Right: 2050

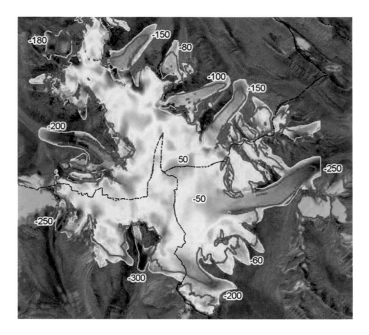

Columbia Icefield 1920–2000: Elevation Change (m)
Yellow = 1920; red = 2000; black = water divide

Supervised by Dr. Brian Menounos, Christina Tennant recalculated the current area of the Columbia Icefield. Most of the contemporary literature had put the figure at around 325 km²; Tennant estimated it to be about 223 km² as of 2005. Depending on exactly what ice masses are technically deemed to be included as part of its mass, and the extent of detached ice not included in the estimates, the Columbia Icefield may be seen to have lost as much as a third of the area that had been ascribed to it in the 1990s. As this illustration shows, parts of the icefield have also diminished considerably in depth. Further research is presently being undertaken at the Columbia Icefield to more accurately determine both its exact area and volume. COURTESY OF CHRISTINA TENNANT, WESTERN CANADIAN CRYOSPHERIC NETWORK

325 square kilometres. Dr. Marshall is not sure at what time the Columbia may have covered such an area, but the work of Dr. Menounos and his colleagues estimated the area to have been about 223 square kilometres as of 2005. In other words, the Columbia Icefield has lost almost a third of the area ascribed to it in the 1990s. We don't yet know its volume, but that number too may soon be forthcoming.

Glacier ice: water in the bank

The realization that some 300 glaciers disappeared along the Great Divide of the Canadian Rockies between 1920 and 1985 did not come as a surprise to researchers. It is not their job to be surprised. Their immediate concern related to ensuring that the analyses were properly conducted and that the findings would stand up to further scientific scrutiny. In the long-standing tradition of the scientific method, it was important that these findings become a sound foundation for further research. Dr. Shawn Marshall's work on the state and future of Alberta's glaciers demonstrated how science builds upon itself to address serious questions such as those related to the effect climate may have on future water supply in the Canadian West.

In many ways, the work of Dr. Marshall and his colleagues at the University of Calgary is a culmination of what had been collectively gained by linked research networks. Marshall's work builds on data already presented by Brian Menounos, Roger Wheate, Matt Beedle and Tobias Bolch, who compared glacial extent measurements in the western cordilleran region between 1985 and 2005 as revealed by Landsat analysis. Their work, in tandem with research by Mike Demuth of the Geological Survey of Canada and by Garry Clarke and Joe Shea at the University of British Columbia, indicated that the total area of glacier cover in the nine regions of the cordillera, including the wilderness areas outside the mountain national parks, diminished by a total of 3057 square kilometres between 1985 and 2005. While glaciologists have yet to come out and say it, these findings are a major blow to the established myth of limitless abundance of water in Canada. We may have 20 per cent of the world's freshwater resources, but much of that is water left "on deposit in the bank" after the last ice age. That ice, as WC²N has clearly demonstrated, is disappearing quickly. Global warming is causing a cryospheric meltdown not dissimilar to an economic collapse. The amount of water that is left in our account in the glacier bank is much less than we expected. Unaccounted-for greenhouse gases are eroding the principal; interest rates are dropping; and the amount is becoming smaller all the time. The disappearance of the major glacial masses in the Canadian Rockies will mean there will be less water in our rivers in late summer throughout the West. What we do not know is how much ice is now buried under collapsed moraines or entrained under debris. This research does suggest, however, that these glaciers are on the way out

Dr. Shawn Marshall is one of the most respected glaciologists and climate scientists in North America. His research has demonstrated the range of effects which loss of the glaciers of the Rocky Mountains could have on the Canadian West by 2100.

and that the pulse of melt we expected as a result of rapid warming has come and gone.

These projections offer important insight into what is happening to water we used to have in the bank in the North and in the mountain West. As renowned hydrologist John Pomeroy has said, what is happening to our glaciers is of great importance to the future climate of the mountain West. While glaciers may not be as significant in terms of total water supply as they were when they were larger, what is happening to glaciers may be a warning of other significant threats. We already know that long before global warming has finished reducing the length and depth of our glaciers it will already be after our mountain snowpacks, and that could have a huge influence on our water supply.

Reduced flows in western rivers will impact power generation and agricultural, industrial and municipal water security throughout the region. These flow reductions will also affect interprovincial water-sharing arrangements and transboundary agreements with the United States such as the Columbia River Treaty.

Beyond creating powerful images of why we need to act on the climate change threat, Garry Clarke and his colleagues in the Western Canadian Cryospheric Network make an articulate and forceful case for why further research – into increasingly accurate modelling parameters that would enable more reliable prediction of future hydrological and climatic states – is crucial to the very survival of our current economic and political structures. That research is slowly advancing.

The next step in research aimed at assessing the future of Alberta's glaciers involved estimating the volume of the ice that still remains on the eastern side of the Rockies. This is not an easy thing to do. Marshall and his University of Calgary colleague Eric White overcame the problem by employing a suite of algorithms to arrive at an average figure of between 30 and 115 cubic kilometres. For the purposes of their first-order assessment, they estimated an average of 42 cubic kilometres. This became the foundation for rough calculations of how long the remaining ice would last in each of Alberta's mountain river basins, based on climate warming trends witnessed over the past 40 years.

The foundation for these estimates was the mass balance history of Peyto Glacier, which is the only glacier in the Rockies for which there is a data record of changes in volume in response to the rising temperatures of the past four decades. Mass balance is defined as the difference between how much snow falls in the accumulation zone and the amount of ice that melts during the warm months in any given year.

While Peyto Glacier currently covers about 12 square kilometres, it has lost 70 per cent of its volume in the last 100 years. Winter snow depth and duration of cover have been declining since the 1970s.

Using a variety of modelling scenarios as a means of anticipating the future, Marshall and White projected the mass balance of Peyto Glacier forward to the end of the 21st century. The results revealed a dramatic decline in volume and runoff from the glacier over time.

After projecting the future of Peyto Glacier forward a century, Marshall then extrapolated the results onto surrounding glacier-fed river basins so as to predict changes in the volume of glaciers feeding the Bow, Red

A Geological Survey of Canada researcher checks snow depth on the Peyto in order to calculate the glacier's current mass balance, or the difference between how much snow has fallen in the accumulation zone versus how much has been lost due to melting during the warm months. A positive mass balance means the glacier will grow or at least stay the same size. A negative mass balance means the glacier is shrinking.

Deer, North Saskatchewan, Athabasca and Peace rivers. The results suggest dramatic loss of glacial ice at the headwaters of each of these systems.

Dr. Marshall then went on to translate the loss of glacial mass at these headwaters into impacts on streamflow over the coming century. These calculations indicated a substantial negative effect on streamflows over time. Dr. Marshall noted that current glacial contribution to Alberta's mountain rivers was in the order of 1.2 cubic kilometres a year. He estimated that as this century progresses this volume will be reduced to as little as 0.66 cubic kilometres a year, or about half. This does not mean, however, that glaciers will lose their importance to the hydrology of the West. In parts of Alberta, existing water resources are fully allocated, if not over-allocated. Further reductions in flows as a result of loss of our mountain glaciers will be noticed by those whose reliable supply of water is suddenly no longer available.

But given current trends, even the 0.66 cubic kilometres contributed by much-diminished glaciers could ultimately be reduced to zero over time. Marshall reasoned that if in fact the volume of existing glaciers was around 45 cubic kilometres as estimated by his primitive methods – and if current temperature trends persisted – then Bow Glacier would completely disappear in 53 years, or somewhere around 2060. Similarly, the ice at the headwaters of the North Saskatchewan would disappear in 72 years, or around 2070, and the glacial sources of the Athabasca would be gone in 83 years, *circa* 2080. Only the glaciers at the headwaters of the Peace and the Red Deer would survive into the next century. Because they are located in high, north-facing cirques, the glaciers feeding the Peace might survive 97 years, and those in the high mountains at the headwaters of the Red Deer might last 132 years.

Marshall noted that the greatest uncertainty in these calculations is the accuracy of present-day ice-volume estimates. As mentioned earlier, his research team put the figure at somewhere between 30 and 110 cubic kilometres. Marshall is concerned that his average projection of between 40 and 50 cubic kilometres may be too low. He went on to say, however, that the volume of glacier ice in the Alberta Rockies was indeed 40 to 50 cubic kilometres at present and that his forecast is for shrinkage of 5 to 10 cubic kilometres by 2100. This would represent a 90 per cent loss of the volume of ice currently present in Alberta's Rockies.

Dr. Marshall made it very clear to his colleagues that these estimates were based only on "first-order" calculations that have not been verified by more accurate measures of the volume of ice that actually exists in Alberta's Rockies. Such more accurate numbers – including far better estimates of how much ice remained concealed under moraines or debris-covered surfaces – would be needed to test the validity of Marshall's projections of the future state of Alberta's glaciers. That work was undertaken by a team led by Mike Demuth of the Geological Survey of Canada.

The Columbia Icefield Research Initiative

As we have seen, the biggest challenge to properly assessing how much water is stored in the glaciers in the western and northern cordillera regions is the problem of accurately determining the volume of existing glacial masses. It is relatively easy to measure area. Volume is far more difficult because it is hard to know the nature of the landforms beneath the ice, and that is what determines the volume of ice that can exist in any given place. Because there is no simple and inexpensive way to do this, many of the projections regarding the state of Canada's remaining glaciers are only rough guesses based on the best information available about the general nature of the topography of Canada's mountain regions. That is why the Geological Survey, in association with Parks Canada, funded the necessary research to accurately determine the volume of ice.

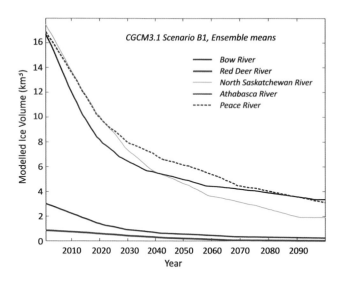

Projected declines in the flow of five major western Canadian rivers as a consequence of loss of glacial ice by the end of the 21st century. IMAGE COURTESY OF DR. SHAWN MARSHALL, UNIVERSITY OF CALGARY

The Columbia Icefield Research Initiative was established in 2010 as a multilateral program of observational and research science to measure the icefield's mass balance. One of its accomplishments has been to develop a monitoring site at the Columbia Icefield that will eventually replace the historically important one on the now rapidly disappearing Peyto Glacier. For the time being at least, the Peyto still flows down from the Wapta Icefield, but sooner or later its monitoring site will be left with little of importance to measure. Until then, the findings from these two sites together will assist in representing regional glacier changes as part of

Mike Demuth checking GPS coordinates at a remote site by an unnamed glacier flowing from the Columbia Icefield.

the GSC's reference glacier and climate observing system and its contribution to the World Glacier Monitoring Service.

The initiative continues at the time of this writing with four active government–university collaborations studying a variety of phenomena such as snow–ice accumulation and ablation at multiple scales and also developing techniques and placing instrumentation to measure, understand and predict the icefield's mass balance and volume changes, ultimately to better assess the water and ecological services it provides.

If this project is permitted to continue, the volume of the Columbia Icefield system will not be merely approximated, as it has been in the past, by estimating volume as a function of area. Instead the volume of ice will be calculated directly and exactly through the use of ground-penetrating radar surveys conducted on the surface of the icefield and through a remote sensing technology called LiDAR. LiDAR is short for light detection and radar. Its operating principles are similar to those of its predecessor technology, RaDAR, which is short for radio detection and ranging (and which, through more than a half-century of use, has become a word familiar enough to be spelled lower-case). With LiDAR, however, the radio microwaves typical of radar are replaced by near-infrared pulses emitted by a laser. This laser energy interacts with surface features, and upon scattering, returns to a detector. The range to the surface is a simple "time of flight" measurement, with the position of the survey aircraft accurately known using the global positioning system.

The aircraft carrying the LiDAR system flies over the study area, capturing information in swaths. Careful analysis of the data yields an illuminated relief map detailing all the features of the landscape and their exact distances from one another. The combination of LiDAR and ground-penetrating radar is expected to yield the first truly accurate measurement of the form and thickness of the Columbia Icefield and how much ice it contains, from which the water equivalent of that ice can be derived. Using these calculations it will then be possible to predict with a fair degree of accuracy how long individual glaciers and even the Columbia Icefield itself may last under a number of projected climate change scenarios.

Given the central position of the Columbia Icefield at the headwaters of three of the country's most important river systems, the Columbia Icefield Research

Initiative could generate research outcomes that will be of great value in determining how much water will be available to those who live in the West in the future. The initiative has the potential be the most important scientific research project undertaken in a Canadian national park since the park system was created in 1885. A great deal of ice in the West is becoming water. By refining our understanding of the glacier ice at the hydrologic apex of western Canada, this research could very well define the state and fate of the entire West. Out of this research we might learn the hydrological limits of the dry West. We may be able to better understand what the western landscape can support, for it is water, not just natural resources, that ultimately constrains sustainability on the Great Plains. There is some urgency in doing so.

Mike Demuth transporting equipment across the Columbia Icefield.
PHOTOGRAPH COURTESY OF THE GLACIOLOGY SECTION OF THE GEOLOGICAL SURVEY OF CANADA

The latest science on deglaciation

In 2015 Dr. Garry Clarke and his colleagues Alexander Jarosch, Faron Anslow, Valentina Radić and Brian Menounos published a paper in *Science*, one of the most prestigious scientific journals in the world, that employed much-improved and far more accurate models to build on earlier estimations of projected deglaciation of western Canada in the 21st century. The results demonstrate that we can, on average, expect to lose about 70 per cent of the glacial ice that existed in Canada's western mountains in 2005 by 2100. The effects will be greatest in the Interior Ranges of British Columbia and in the Rocky Mountains. Less affected will be the coastal tidewater glaciers in northern British Columbia and Alaska. We can expect coastal glaciers to be diminished by 65 per cent to 85 per cent and glaciers in the Interior Ranges and the Rocky Mountains to suffer volume and area losses in some cases of up to 90 per cent or more. The main effects of deglaciation will be associated with changes in the hydrological cycle and consequent impacts on water availability which will affect hydr electric power generation, recreation and tourism. If current trends persist, we can expect the Canadian West to be a very different place by the end of the century.

Why it's important to keep the climate cold

Many visitors to the Columbia Icefield ask why keeping this region cold even matters. If these glaciers are going to disappear anyway, what difference will further scientific research make? The answer is that we don't know enough about what is happening to ice and snow in the high Rockies to be able to predict the future. Because our temperature records are almost all from elevations between 640 and 1340 metres, it is suspected that current extrapolations are probably underestimating warming at higher altitudes.

The camp of the Columbia Icefield research project is on a plateau at about 3200 m elevation, just below the summit of Snow Dome. The team's first significant discovery was clear evidence of substantial midwinter melt, probably from high temperatures experienced everywhere in the mountain West in 2010, the year the survey began. Winter melt at high altitude in the Rockies had been predicted by many climate models, and this confirmation of it is troubling because it suggests that ice masses and glaciers will be under attack, not just from below by warming in the valleys but also from above due to warmer winter air temperatures. This does not mean, however, that conditions on the Columbia Icefield are always pleasant. While the region around the Columbia may be warming, the high reaches of the icefield itself can still be a very cold and treacherous place. Researchers have been pinned down for days here by the very snowfall they were studying, and they are often unsure when the weather will clear enough to airlift their camp to the valley floor. PHOTO COURTESY OF SASHA CHICHAGOV, GEOLOGICAL SURVEY OF CANADA

It is at these elevations that climate change effects are expected to be felt first and to be most pronounced in terms of their impacts on water supply. At the moment, we simply don't know how much faster warming may be occurring at higher altitudes, because we have few measures and no baseline for comparison. As noted, we don't know enough about what implications this may have for water supply for cities and farms that rely on rivers that originate in the Columbia Icefield and other icefields and glaciers in Canada's western mountains.

The long-term ecological effects of widespread glacial recession and diminution of snowpack and snow cover are also little known. We should expect, however, that the reduction in the amount of light reflected by ice and snow in this region will have further warming effects on climate and that these impacts will also cascade through both terrestrial and aquatic ecosystems.

With the decrease in the extent and influence of glaciers, our rivers are already warming, which will affect every cold-sensitive species, from the smallest diatom and pathogen to every kind of fish. We have already seen what consistently warmer winters do in terms of insect infestations. Higher winter temperatures have aided the advance of forest pests like the pine bark beetle, which has now spread through about 10 million hectares of British Columbia forest. Some 411 million cubic feet of commercial wood has already been destroyed, which amounts to twice the annual harvest of all the logging in Canada.

With warmer temperatures and longer, hotter summers we will also have to pay more attention to water's diametric and symbolic opposite, fire. Dr. Mike

Flannigan and his colleagues at Natural Resources Canada have been able to predict the effects that increased carbon dioxide concentrations will have on the length of the fire season in boreal forests. This important work suggests that the season will increase from 10 days to a whopping 50 days over much of the Canadian boreal. Based on carbon dioxide increases alone, Flannigan and his colleagues predict an outsized 75 to 120 per cent increase in the area burned each year by the end of the century.

We are already beginning to witness climate change impacts on vegetation and wildlife, especially in the alpine. For the last century, the alpine tundra zone has been defined as those places having a mean annual temperature of between 8 and 9.5°C during the warmest months of the year. The early 21st century has already seen temperatures rising above 10°C in large areas of the North American alpine tundra climate zone.

By this measure it has been determined that 73 per cent of the alpine tundra in the western United States can no longer be classified as such. This means that since 1987, the continental US has lost three-quarters of its alpine regions to global warming. As we have seen, it is not unreasonable to anticipate that rising temperatures are having a similar effect on mountains in Canada.

As the climate grows warmer a thermal sea will rise up the slopes of our national parks islands, separating each mountain range farther from the next. This will aggravate precisely the two conditions that the theory of island biogeography suggests will deplete species diversity: species will become more isolated and their habitats will shrink.

Pika

The pika, or rock rabbit as it is sometimes known, is a species that lives only in the alpine regions of North America's western mountains. As ethologist Anthony Barnosky explains, pika tend to die of heat stress if they are caught outside in temperatures above 25.5°C for any length of time, which explains why they are generally found only near mountaintops. In the Colorado Rockies the temperature tends to cool by 2°C for every 300-metre gain in elevation. By going higher, pika avoid the heat of the valley floor.

Over the last 50 years, however, lethal temperatures have been moving upslope, pushing the pika ever upward. The problem for pika in Colorado is that they are now reaching the summits of mountains only to find that rising temperatures make it impossible to survive even there. The higher latitudes and altitudes of the northern Rockies may be the last stand for this species.

The pika is actually a member of the rabbit family, but because it lives in a cold environment and remains active under the snow during winter, its ears are smaller and rounder than what we would expect of a rabbit. What researchers have discovered is that while the pika is a cold-hardy mountain species, it has limited tolerance for warming temperatures.

Marmot

The writing may also be on the wall for the marmot, at least in the southern Rockies. As naturalists have observed, marmots construct elaborate burrow systems into which, in the Colorado Rockies, they disappear whenever the outside temperature falls below 1°C or gets hotter than 26°C. It is interesting to note that marmots have tolerance levels that embrace both ends of the temperature spectrum, which we now know is common to many alpine species. In a marmot burrow, the temperature stays between 8°C and 10°C, even though the outside temperature may be higher or lower. Marmots spend 60 per cent of their lives in hibernation. Marmots emerge from hibernation sometime in the spring, just as the fat reserves they packed on during the previous summer are exhausted.

US researcher Anthony Barnosky found that, on average, marmots in Colorado were emerging from their burrows some 23 days – nearly a full month – earlier than they were in the 1970s. Barnosky also discovered that in Colorado at least, more winter snow is falling each year and even increasing spring temperatures cannot melt it fast enough to permit plant growth to occur before the marmots end their annual hibernation. As Barnosky describes it, starving marmots in Colorado are coming out of hibernation to discover that the salad bar isn't open and won't open for some time – and then they are dying. The climate change circumstance marmots are presently facing is different from what has occurred in the past, at least in the southern Rockies. This may also be the case for other hibernating animals, including bears. Whether

The hoary marmot can be found in the alpine regions below the Columbia Icefield. It is the largest member of the squirrel family and uniquely adapted to living at high altitudes within very narrow regimes of temperature. The marmot can hibernate up to nine months of the year, which makes it vulnerable to changing climatic conditions and plant availability when it comes out of hibernation.

snowfall patterns as they are trending at the time of this writing will persist in a rapidly changing American southwest remains to be seen, but what is already clear is that the future will be different than the present.

Though we may not be worried about pika or marmots in Banff or Jasper National Park at the moment, all the alarms are going off with respect to caribou survival. The mountain caribou has already been extirpated from Banff National Park and there are concerns about its survival throughout the Canadian Rocky Mountain Parks World Heritage Site. Ultimately, with no place to go, upwardly advancing cold-hardy refugees

While mountain caribou are still seen occasionally in the Columbia Icefield area, their habitat has been diminishing throughout their North American range. While habitat disruption – by development in and around the very parks that were created specifically to protect such living wonders – has been a big factor in this species' decline, a changing climate is also adding to the stress. This female has dropped one of her antlers.

Rocky Mountain bighorn sheep are common in the Columbia Icefield area, where they are often seen licking road salt off the pavement of the Icefields Parkway. Though both males and females have horns, the annual growth of rams' horns often determines social hierarchy in a species where horn size can play a big role in mating success.

The mountain goat is a true alpine species. Often found on the steepest and highest of mountains, it can actually be seen looking down on the Columbia Icefield from vantages which humans would find very difficult to reach. Like the Rocky Mountain bighorn, however, the mountain goat lacks certain minerals and salts in its high-altitude diet, and as a consequence it can be found in the valley at natural salt licks along the Icefields Parkway.

perish. Suddenly we see that our old land and wildlife management ideas no longer apply, because our fundamental conservation goals have been made self-contradictory by climate change.

The first question, at least in terms of wildlife protection, then becomes: How can we protect species whose last stronghold in protected areas like those represented by the Columbia Icefield is threatened by

It is not just animals that are affected by rapid changes in climate. Mountain forests are advancing upward in altitude amid warming conditions, and alpine plant communities are being pushed upward ahead of the trees. In spectacular alpine meadows such as those on Parker Ridge and in Wilcox Pass it is possible to witness the extraordinary cold-hardiness of alpine flowering plants. The alpine buttercup, for example, blooms right through the melting spring snow.

climate change? The second question is: What are we trying to keep whole in ecologically protected areas?

The action plan that has to be on the ground where large, relatively intact natural systems still exist may boil down to three verbs: keep, connect and create. This, it appears, is as good as any place for us to begin. We need to keep and protect what we have preserved in our parks and World Heritage sites. We need to connect what we have already protected to corridors and spaces outside of our national parks. And then we have to expand protection to those corridors to ensure that as many species as possible can move northward and upward along with the temperature regimes and ecosystems they rely on for their survival. But this cannot be done without an understanding of what is happening to the ice and snow that are central determinants of the character of ecosystems in cold regions.

We know now that snow cover, atmospheric circulation and temperature are interdependent and relate to one another as feedbacks. Water and temperature define climate, climate defines ecosystems, and ecosystems define us. In the absence of ice and snow we would be different people living in a different world. It appears that in the context of where and how we live in Canada, cold really does matter. And now we are beginning to understand why.

Climate, Water and the Ideal of National Parks

Changes in global hydro-climatic circumstances create an opportunity to rethink the value and mandate of our national parks and protected places. The Canadian Rocky Mountain Parks World Heritage Site encompasses four national parks, three provincial parks, 13 national historic sites and four Canadian heritage rivers. Within the World Heritage Site there are no fewer than 27 mountain ranges, 669 prominent peaks, 12 major icefields and some 384 glaciers.

These mountains are the water tower of the West. This combined reserve encompasses a total 44 rivers and 164 named tributaries, only two of which are dammed. Four of the greatest rivers on the continent are born here. Within its boundaries are some 295 lakes and thousands of ponds, ephemeral pools and wetlands.

What has also become clear is that just curbing greenhouse gas emissions will not be enough to restore climatic stability. We can no longer ignore the local value of natural ecosystem processes. In order to gain even partial rein over the hydrological cycle we have to enlist all the help nature can provide us. We gain that help by protecting and restoring critical aquatic ecosystem function locally and by reversing land and soil degradation wherever we can.

Athabasca Falls, downstream of the Columbia Icefield, in Jasper National Park, during the peak of the spring melt. The fact that the Columbia Icefield forms the headwaters of three of the great rivers of the Pacific Northwest has yet to be fully appreciated in the way we value our national parks. Once again, what we have protected may now protect us in a changing climate.

No one knows better than those who manage our national parks that the watershed basin is the minimum unit at which water must managed. This fact in itself – that basin-scale water management is critical to social, economic and environmental resilience under changing hydro-climatic conditions – should inspire our actions.

We already changed the world once by doing the right thing in creating the protected areas system we now have in Canada's western mountains. I believe we have it in us to do the right thing again by using this system as a foundation for the creation of a new water ethic in Canada and, through example, the world. Our appreciation and understanding of the Columbia Icefield, and the changes we are seeing take place there with respect to the most precious of all our natural resources, could be the inspiration for that new national water ethic.

Through reaffirmation of the link between water and our national identity a second great public policy achievement in the West could be built upon the first. We have created the Canadian Rocky Mountain Parks World Heritage Site and protected the surrounding areas. Now let's use what we have done to demonstrate to the world how we can follow the water in our protected rivers and lakes back to the headwaters of our history. From there we can identify that point in time where we made a wrong turn in terms of understanding the true value of our land and water resources. Correcting that mistake and starting again downstream toward meaningful sustainability demands that we decide what steady state we want for water and climate and then set self-regulation on the road to achieving that state.

Glossary: The language of place

alpine: the life zone in mountainous regions that extends above treeline. In the Canadian Rockies, treeline historically ranged from about 2100–2250 metres, or roughly 6900–7400 feet above sea level, depending on slope and exposure. But with warming conditions, treeline is slowly advancing both northward geographically and upward in altitude. Life does extend above the treeline, however, usually in the form of high meadows composed of interconnected low-lying rafts of plant life. The alpine life zone in the Canadian Rockies is also referred to as alpine tundra, for in many ways conditions of life in this zone represent a southward extension, due to high altitude, of the polar climate conditions that have created the tundra of the Arctic.

alpine valley glacier: a small mountain glacier fed by accumulation of snow in the same trough in which it flows.

Anthropocene: the geological epoch many scientists believe we have entered as a consequence of the fact that human activities now rival the processes of nature itself. Unlike earlier epochs in the earth's history brought about by meteorite strikes and other geological events that resulted in mass extinctions, this epoch is marked by our own overall impact on the Earth system. Climate disruption is only one of the Earth system boundaries that mark the safe zone we must stay within if we want a prosperous future. By virtue of our numbers and our activities we have altered global carbon, nitrogen and phosphorous cycles. We are causing changes in the chemistry, salinity and temperature of our oceans and the composition of our atmosphere. Changes in the composition of the atmosphere in tandem with land-use modifications and our growing water demands have also altered the global water cycle. The cumulative measure of the extent to which we have crossed these boundaries is the rate of biodiversity loss.

bergschrund: large, semi-permanent crevasse at the head of a glacier which separates the moving ice from stagnant ice or from the rock surface adjacent.

Carboniferous: a period of the Palaeozoic Era in the earth's history. It occurred between the end of the Devonian Period approximately 360 million years ago and the beginning of the Permian about 300 million years ago. During this period coal beds were laid down as central features of the stratigraphy of many parts of the northern hemisphere. The Carboniferous is often broken down into two geological periods in North America: the Mississippian followed by the Pennsylvanian.

Cenozoic: the most recent geological era in the earth's history, extending from roughly 65.5 million years ago to the present (if recognized as such, the Anthropocene will be defined as an epoch, which is of shorter duration than a larger era, in which an epoch is but a part). This geological era includes the Paleogene and Neogene periods. Much of the glaciation that shaped the Canadian Rockies as we know them today occurred during this era.

continental divide: a divide is a height of land separating two watersheds, and a continental divide separates watersheds that flow into different oceans. In the case of the Canadian Rockies, the Continental Divide, or Great Divide as it is often called, separates waters flowing into the Pacific Ocean from those bound for the Atlantic. At the Columbia Icefield there is a rare triple continental divide, which is the high point on Snow Dome that separates waters flowing into the Atlantic, Pacific and Arctic oceans.

Cretaceous: a geological period in the history of the earth that extended from roughly 145 to 66 million years ago and is marked by the wholesale disappearance of many of the planet's earlier life forms, including most dinosaurs.

crevasse: a crack or fissure in glacial ice. A crevasse is a break in ice, whereas a crevice is a narrow opening resulting from a split or crack in rock.

firn line: the often quite obvious boundary on the upper reaches of a glacier above which winter snow does not melt. The firn line distinguishes where a glacier ends and where the icefield that forms it begins.

geology: the science that deals with the earth's physical structure and substance, its history, and the processes that act on it.

glacier: a body of permanent snow that has been compressed by its own weight into ice that has begun to move under the influence of gravity.

graupel: granular snow pellets, sometimes called soft hail.

Great Glaciation: a major glacial period that began in

North America some 240,000 years ago, and appears to have lasted approximately 100,000 years.

hoar: a sparkling, crystalline form of frost on, above or below the snow surface. Depth hoar is recrystallized snow found in the bottom layers of the snowpack. It is this recrystallization at the base of the snowpack that can make steep snow slopes unstable, triggering avalanches. Avalanches are very common in the Columbia Icefield area well into the spring.

hypothermia: the condition of having an abnormally low body temperature which can bring on death.

icecap: a glacial mass forming on an extensive area of relatively level land and flowing outward from its centre. A mountain icecap is a flat or gently sloping alpine upland buried in ice.

"Ice Explorer": a custom-built, 56-passenger, rubber-tired vehicle developed specifically for travel on Athabasca Glacier at the Columbia Icefield which is now being used in other glacial environments as well. The original name of the Ice Explorer was "Snocoach," which was a contraction of "snow" and "coach" that was used to market the Athabasca Glacier experience.

icefield: an area less than 50,000 square kilometres of permanent snow undergoing the processes of compressing itself under its weight into ice, which flows downhill in the form of glaciers.

ice worms: small annelid worms of the genus *Mesenchytraeus* that spend their life cycles within or on glacial ice. First discovered in Alaska in 1887, they were made famous by a poem written by Robert Service entitled

"The Ballad of the Ice-Worm Cocktail." Research indicates that these worms are among the most remarkably cold-hardy species in the world. But they can stand only cold, not heat: it appears that when ice worms are exposed to temperatures as high as 5°C, their membrane structures disassociate, causing the worms to liquefy or "melt." Though not common in the Rockies, ice worms are known to exist abundantly in some areas of the North Cascade Range in British Columbia and Washington.

Little Ice Age: a period of cooling from about 1300 CE to about 1850 CE during which glaciers in the northern hemisphere, including those in the Canadian Rockies, appear to have advanced significantly.

millwell: a vertical hole through which surface water is carried down into a glacier. Some millwells are deep enough to carry meltwater right to the base of the ice. A millwell is the same as a moulin, or glacier mill.

moraine: a deposit of rock debris carried and shaped by glacial flow and erosion. Several types of moraines are found on and around Athabasca Glacier and in the Columbia Icefield region. These include lateral, terminal, medial and ablation moraines, each of which is formed by the dynamics of different kinds of glacial action.

moulin. See **millwell**.

ogives: a regular pattern of undulating bands of dark and light ice on the surface of a steeply descending glacier. These often evenly spaced bands bend downglacier because the glacier moves faster at its centre than it does on its edges. The dark bands are composed of ice that moved over the icefall down which the glacier is pouring during the summer season. The light bands are composed of ice that moved over the icefall during the winter.

Ordovician: a geological period in the earth's history extending from about 488 million years ago to about 443 million years ago. During the Ordovician, the continents of the southern hemisphere coalesced into a single continent called Gondwana, which slowly began to drift toward the South Pole. During the same period, the continents Laurentia (present-day North America), Siberia and Baltica (present-day northern Europe) were still separate continents. Fossil fish have been discovered from this period and, on land, the preserved remains of mosses.

outlet valley glacier: a glacier, such as the Athabasca, that flows out of a major icefield accumulation zone and into a neighbouring valley.

pink snow: spring snow turned pink or red by the algae known as *Chlamydomonas nivalis*. Creatures that thrive at or below the freezing point of water are known as cryophiles. There are a lot more of these species than anyone suspected. A 1968 study reported the presence of 466 species of microorganisms found in snow, of which 77 were fungi and 35 were bacteria. The remainder are algae. The best known cryophiles found in the Columbia Icefield area of the Rocky Mountains are the red algae found in snow in concentrations large enough to turn the spring and summer snowpack pink. For many of these organisms, optimal growth can only occur at temperatures below 10°C. In some strains of snow algae, particularly *Chlamydomonas nivalis*, which is most common here, optimal growth of motile vegetative cells occurs at temperatures between 1°C and 5°C. The very upper limit of temperature at which growth can occur in many of these species is between 16°C and 20°C. Minimal temperature for growth is 0°C or even lower. It is the survivability of these algae at extremely cold temperatures that is truly spectacular. In laboratory tests, viable cells of snow algae have recovered from temperatures as low as −196°C.

rock flour: rock that has been ground into fine powder by glacial ice. This fine debris gives a milky colour to rivers and, depending on concentration, a brown colour to lakes fed by glaciers. The suspension of rock flour in many of the lakes in the Columbia Icefield region is of just the right concentration, however, to make the water seem to glow turquoise. The dazzling blue of Peyto Lake and Lake Louise as seen from above is caused by rock flour suspended in their waters.

sérac: a standing tower of ice breaking off a glacier as it stretches downslope over an icefall.

solar wind: the great storm of light and radioactive particles through which the earth spins as it passes through the sun's glow.

watermelon snow. See **pink snow.**

watershed: the area drained by a river system, or a ridge dividing the areas drained by different river systems.

Further reading

Historical non-fiction

The only first-hand account of the discovery of the Columbia Icefield that is still in print is found in *Climbs and Exploration in the Canadian Rockies*, by J. Norman Collie and Hugh Stutfield. A modern paperback reprint of this classic, with a new foreword by Gillean Daffern, was published in 2008 by Rocky Mountain Books.

There are two excellent biographies of Norman Collie: William C. Taylor's *The Snows of Yesteryear: J. Norman Collie, Mountaineer* (Toronto: Holt, Rinehart & Winston of Canada, 1973); and Christine Mill's *Norman Collie, A Life in Two Worlds: Mountain Explorer and Scientist, 1859–1942* (Aberdeen University Press, 1987). Dr. Taylor shared material from his book with Mill for hers.

William C. Taylor has also written a very interesting book on the history of the Lovat Scouts, encompassing the training they undertook in the Columbia Icefield area during the Second World War: *Highland Soldiers: The Story of a Mountain Regiment* (Canmore, Alta.: Coyote Books, 1994).

A thorough history of the discovery and later exploration of the Columbia Icefield area can also be found in the present author's *Ecology & Wonder in the Canadian Rocky Mountain Parks World Heritage Site* (Edmonton: Athabasca University Press, 2010).

A vast range of historical materials concerning the Columbia Icefield area can be found in the archives of the Whyte Museum of the Canadian Rockies in Banff and in the Jasper–Yellowhead Museum in Jasper.

Historical fiction

Thomas Wharton's *Icefields* (NeWest Press, 1995) is spare and simple, like the glaciers and frozen peaks he describes, mirroring the beauty of the high alpine landscape. Only the important features relating to the nature of place stand out. Wharton's characters are similarly constructed, reduced to the elemental spareness of the ice over which they wander, subject to only the most fundamental emotions. We see the novel's characters come to grips with themselves by coming to grips with the ice, rock and pure light of the icefield upon which this remarkable tale unfolds. It is not often that you come across a locally written classic. Not since Sid Marty's *Men for the Mountains* (Toronto: McClelland & Stewart, 1978) has the theme of Jasper mountains been handled with such clarity and eloquence.

Scientific work

Demuth, Mike. *Becoming Water: Glaciers in a Warming World.* Calgary: Rocky Mountain Books, 2012.

Demuth, M.N., D.S. Munro and G.J. Young, eds. *Peyto Glacier: One Century of Science.* Saskatoon: National Water Research Institute, 2006.

Luckman, Brian, and Trudy Kavanagh. "Impact of climate fluctuations on mountain environments in the Canadian Rockies." *Ambio* 29, no. 7 (November 2000): 371–380. Reprint (pdf) accessed 2016-03-07 at http://is.gd/Vm2l2y.

O'Riordan, Jon, and Robert William Sandford. *The Climate Nexus: Water, Food, Energy and Biodiversity in a Changing World*. Calgary: Rocky Mountain Books, 2015.

Sandford, Robert William. *Cold Matters: The State and Fate of Canada's Fresh Water*. Calgary: Rocky Mountain Books, 2012.

————. *Storm Warning: Water and Climate Security in a Changing World*. Calgary: Rocky Mountain Books, 2015.

Acknowledgements

The author wishes to acknowledge the support of Dr. John Pomeroy, director of the Centre for Hydrology at the University of Saskatchewan, without whose generous sharing of knowledge, tireless commitment to increasing public awareness of ice-, snow- and climate-related water matters this book would not have been possible. The author would like to further acknowledge that this book would have little if any substance without the cooperation of all the scientists who contributed to this work. I am deeply honoured and grateful for their support. Special recognition in this regard must go to doctors Shawn Marshall, Garry Clarke, Brian Luckman, Brian Menounos, Al Pietroniro and David Sauchyn and of course to my good friend Mike Demuth of the glaciology section of the Geological Survey of Canada.

The author also wishes to particularly acknowledge the assistance of Peter Lemieux and his staff at Athabasca Glacier Icewalks for their productive, ongoing discussions about Athabasca Glacier and for their always generous professional courtesy.

The project benefited in its final stages from the support of the author's colleagues at the United Nations University Institute for Water, Environment and Health.

The author also wishes to gratefully acknowledge the support and thoughtful assistance of Ralph Sliger, who, as president and chief pilot of Rockies Heli Canada, made a special effort on each of our annual aerial surveys to get us safely to where we needed to go in weather that allowed us to optimize our observations.

Special thanks are also due to Rocky Mountain Books and in particular to publisher Don Gorman for his commitment to books on water and climate; to editor Joe Wilderson for his diligence, intelligence, patience and good humour; and to art director Chyla Cardinal, whose mindful designs make books like this shine.

And of course, it must be acknowledged that the author alone takes full responsibility for any errors, omissions, misperceptions or misunderstandings the book may contain. Understanding the state and fate of Canada's glaciers and predicting the future of the Columbia Icefield are not likely to get easier any time soon.

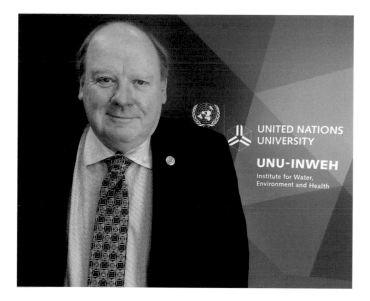

About the author

Robert William Sandford is the EPCOR Chair for Water and Climate Security at the United Nations University Institute for Water, Environment and Health. In this capacity he was the co-author of the UN *Water in the World We Want* report on post-2015 global sustainable development goals relating to water.

In his work Bob is committed to translating scientific research outcomes into language decision makers can use to craft timely and meaningful public policy, and to bringing international example to bear on local water issues. To this end, Bob is also senior adviser on water issues for the Interaction Council, a global public policy forum composed of more than 30 former heads of government including Jean Chrétien of Canada,

Bill Clinton of the US and Gro Harlem Brundtland of Norway.

Bob is also a Fellow of the Centre for Hydrology at the University of Saskatchewan and a Fellow of the Biogeoscience Institute at the University of Calgary. He is a senior policy adviser for the Adaptation to Climate Change team at Simon Fraser University and is also a member of the Forum for Leadership on Water (FLOW), a national water policy research group centred in Toronto. In 2013 *Alberta Ventures* magazine recognized Bob as one of the year's 50 most influential Albertans.

In addition to many other books, Bob is also author or co-author of a number of high-profile works on water, including *Cold Matters: The State and Fate of Canada's Fresh Water*; *Saving Lake Winnipeg*; *Flood Forecast: Climate Risk and Resiliency in Canada*; and *The Columbia River Treaty: A Primer*, all published by Rocky Mountain Books. His two latest books are *The Climate Nexus: Water, Food, Energy and Biodiversity in a Changing World* (with former BC deputy minister of environment Jon O'Riordan) and *Storm Warning: Water and Climate Security in a Changing World*, both published in the fall of 2015 by RMB.

**UNITED NATIONS
UNIVERSITY**

UNU-INWEH

**Institute for Water,
Environment and Health**

The United Nations University Institute for Water, Environment and Health (UNU-INWEH) is a member of the United Nations University family of organisations. It is the UN think tank on water created by the UNU Governing Council in 1996. The mission of the institute is to help resolve pressing water challenges that are of concern to the United Nations, its member states and their people, through knowledge-based synthesis of existing bodies of scientific discovery; through targeted, cutting-edge research that identifies emerging policy issues; through application of on-the-ground, scalable solutions based on credible research; and through relevant and targeted public outreach. The institute is hosted by the Government of Canada and McMaster University.

The designations employed and presentations of material throughout this publication do not imply the expression of any opinion whatsoever on the part of the United Nations University (UNU) concerning the legal status of any country, territory, city or area or of its authorities, or concerning the delimitation of its frontiers or boundaries. The views expressed in this publication are those of the author and do not necessarily reflect the views of the UNU. Mention of the names of firms or commercial products does not imply endorsement by UNU.